SPORTSPERFORMANCE

ROWING

POWER AND ENDURANCE

SUSAN LEZOTTE

CONTEMPORARY
BOOKS, INC.
CHICAGO ▪ NEW YORK

Library of Congress Cataloging-in-Publication Data

Lezotte, Susan.
  Sportsperformance: rowing power and endurance.

  1. Rowing.   2. Rowing—Training.   I. United States
Rowing Association.   II. Title.
GV791.L65   1987   797.1'23   87-15443
ISBN 0-8092-4729-1 (pbk.)

Photography (except where noted) by Terry McClenahan

Published by Contemporary Books, Inc.
180 North Michigan Avenue, Chicago, Illinois 60601
Manufactured in the United States of America
Library of Congress Catalog Card Number: 87-15443
International Standard Book Number: 0-8092-4729-1

Published simultaneously in Canada by Beaverbooks, Ltd.
195 Allstate Parkway, Valleywood Business Park
Markham, Ontario L3R 4T8 Canada

CONTENTS

FOREWORD

Welcome to the world of rowing!

What is it that has brought you here? Or, more importantly, what is it that will keep you here? I have been a rower for over 20 years, with experiences running the gamut from Juniors to collegiate to international to Masters, and I expect I will always be a rower. Despite the undeniably competitive bias of my rowing career, the reasons I started to row, and continue to row, apply to every level of rowing. By describing what motivates me, I hope to encourage you to become involved in rowing.

Rowing is, first and foremost, just plain fun. I know I could never have put in the years of intense training that international competition requires if I didn't on some basic level gain pleasure from the simple fact of being on the water in a small boat.

Setting forth in the early-morning light is an adventure, an exploration of a landscape that even in a city is often quiet, green, and peaceful. If you are fortunate enough to be rowing in a rural setting, the immersion in nature can be complete (especially if you tip over). On the Connecticut

River near Hanover, New Hampshire, you can row for hours without meeting another human being, slicing through the morning fog and unearthly stillness. The signs of civilization are rare, and even they are likely to be farmhouses of another age. Rowing on Lake Chocorua (also in New Hampshire), I once passed within 20 yards of a moose, standing knee-deep in the water-lily shallows. Upon seeing me, it ambled off into the woods, by all appearances less startled than I.

Even on a crowded afternoon on the Schuylkill River in Philadelphia, though, there is a measure of the same quality. The modern-day world and all its concerns are much farther away than a measurement of the distance to the riverbank would suggest. This feeling of peace is accentuated by the very nature of the sensations of rowing. Floating softly on the water, every motion cushioned by the medium through which and on which you move, rowing is silky, smooth, and relaxing. Though these impressions may be forgotten when you are actually racing, without them the preparation for competition would be almost unendurable drudgery.

A second reason for the strength of rowing's appeal is that rowing is an opportunity to experience the rewards, both physical and mental, of hard work in a nonimpact and therefore relatively injury-free environment. I *like* working hard and pushing myself. There is a feeling of satisfaction produced by triumph over my own inclination to avoid discomfort, which less strenuous activities cannot reproduce. In addition, the physiological benefits of rowing, an essentially aerobic activity, are legion. It exercises every major muscle group; arms, legs, and back are all involved, providing complete development.

At one time I made the statement that what I liked about rowing was that you could try as hard as you wanted to hurt yourself, and all that would happen is that you would go faster and get stronger. I was fifteen years old at the time and pretty indestructible, but the point is that rowing is a sport in which you can extend yourself to the limits of physical endurance, and suffer no more lasting harm than a few blisters on your hands. Injuries are rare, and most of them happen *off* the water, lifting weights or running up and down football stadium steps, for example. I have never been hurt by rowing.

A large part of my rowing experience has been competitive, and one of the things that I like about competitive rowing, and that I somehow recognized from the start, was that it is a sport that rewards hard work far more than most. Your success is largely within your control, and is primarily a function of your desire for that success, expressed as a willingness to make whatever sacrifice is necessary, whether in practice or on race day.

Rowing involves the repetition of a single motion, admittedly difficult to perfect but one that most people can get reasonably good at if they practice enough and receive decent instruction. With proper coaching, intelligent training, and lots of hard work almost anyone can excel in the sport.

If you are planning to become involved in a team-boat rowing program, perhaps in fours or eights, you will also have an opportunity to enjoy the special rapport and camaraderie that develops in many crews. The quality of shared experience is stronger in rowing than in many other sports, at least in part because other than the coxswain there are no "positions"—everyone rowing in the boat is going through exactly the same struggle, with the same duties and expectations and the same outcome. You win or lose as a team, and there is no way for an individual to look good in a losing cause. I have always been extremely moved by the closeness that has developed in the crews I have been a part of, and the resulting friendships have lasted, and will last, for a long time. Even in single sculling this feeling can arise in relation to competitors, for win or lose they are the only ones who were really there and who can really know.

Finally, in my twilight years (Over-the-Hill Boat Club, here I come) I have learned to appreciate yet another quality of rowing, one which certainly has nothing to do with my original attraction to the sport. It is the fact that rowing is a sport for a lifetime. You can row at any age (even compete!), you can row with any number of others (including zero), and you can find a place to row *almost* anywhere. At some point you may need a hand carrying your boat down to the water, but maybe that's when it's time to take up golf.

In closing, I return you to my original theme, the one without which all the others could never have been enough. I quote from the Water Rat in Kenneth Grahame's *The Wind in the Willows*:

" 'Nice? It's the *only* thing,' said the Water Rat solemnly, as he leaned forward for his stroke. 'Believe me, my young friend, there is *nothing*—absolutely nothing—half so much worth doing as simply messing about in boats. Simply messing,' he went on dreamily: 'messing—about—in—boats. . . .' "

Happy rowing.

Tiff Wood

ACKNOWLEDGMENTS

The author is grateful to United States Rowing for making this project possible. The author is also indebted to Peggy O'Neal, Eric Stoll, and Tiff Wood, who generously contributed their time and expertise to this book. Special thanks go to the athletes, coaches, and other rowing enthusiasts who shared their knowledge and love of rowing during interviews.

Terry McClenahan, 26, the book's photographer, has been rowing for ten years and photographing for twelve years. He began doing both while at Choate Rosemary Hall School in Wallingford, Connecticut. He majored in photography and rowed as a lightweight at Wesleyan University, where he graduated in 1985. Mr. McClenahan has competed for the Durham Boat Club in New Hampshire and Vesper Boat Club; he has coached rowing at Wesleyan and at St. Joseph's Prep in Philadelphia. He is now a lightweight sculler for Undine Barge Club and head rowing coach at Lower Merion High School.

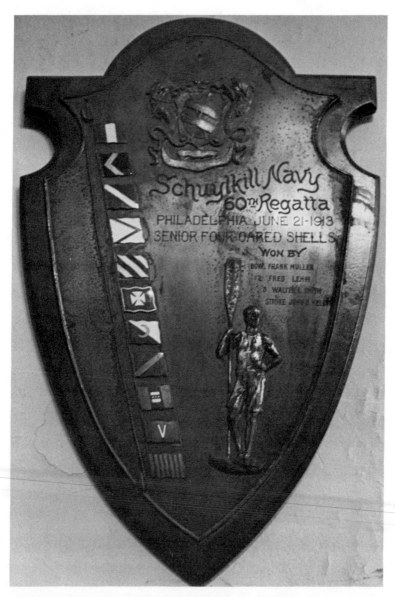

A trophy hanging in the Vesper Boat Club awarded to its victorious four without cox, which won the 60th Schuylkill Navy Regatta. Schuylkill Navy, the oldest amateur sports association in the U.S., governs rowing on the Schuylkill River in Philadelphia. The stroke of the crew was John B. Kelly, father of the late Princess Grace of Monaco and of Jack Kelly, Jr., another rowing legend.

1
HISTORICAL HIGHLIGHTS

Modern rowers enjoy their sport and find it beneficial to their health. You'll understand why the first time you glide across a glassy lake on a perfect fall day. The entrancing water, the incredible blue sky, and the dazzling trees soothe and refresh your mind, while your body unwinds as your arms, legs, and back rhythmically drive the oars through the water and release the day's tensions.

Some of the earliest rowers, the Athenians and Persians, probably didn't get quite as much enjoyment out of rowing and probably questioned its benefit to their health. They usually rowed to exhaustion in life or death battles against each other. Despite being outnumbered, the Athenians usually outrowed their foes. Paintings on ancient pottery revealed that the Athenians rowed on movable slides, while the Persians sat on fixed seats. The sliding seat enables the oarsman to use his entire body in driving the oars, while the fixed seat forces the rower to use arms only.

The stakes in collegiate rowing are much less than those at Marathon. Collegians bet shirts on their races, and losing oarsmen forfeit only their shirts, not their lives. However,

1

competition is still keen and every advantage is sought. Consequently, in the 1800s, the sliding seat was rediscovered by college crews trying to outdo one another. In one of the early races, Harvard oarsmen achieved the sliding seat effect by applying grease to their leather pants and sliding up and down the wooden seat block. This innovation earned them a resounding victory over Yale. As the story goes, the Yale oarsmen countered and won the next year by greasing their trousers with the university's oatmeal. The following year Harvard used seats with wooden rollers to gain victory. The Harvard-Yale rowing contest dates back to 1852 and is the oldest intercollegiate event in America.

Today, rowing is popular in colleges across the country, and collegiate rowing is still an important training ground for America's world-class rowers. Many top American rowers row their first strokes in college. Numerous rowing careers have been launched at freshman orientation, where enthusiastic upperclassmen persuaded incoming athletes to go out for crew. For some freshmen, the initial appeal of crew was that it could be substituted in the curriculum for the required physical education classes.

Many freshmen sign up for crew just to try something new. Athletes also find crew refreshing because it's a total team sport and doesn't glorify the individual. Rather, as world medalist Andy Sudduth explains, "In crew, the speed of the boat is limited by the weakest guy." Every person in the boat does exactly the same thing, and victory goes to the team that best meshes individual talent to achieve a synchronized whole greater than the individual parts. In crew, every team member understands exactly what his or her teammates are feeling. There is no distinction in position, as on a baseball team. Every seat in the boat is expected to row as hard as possible, period. The loyalty and human bonds generated by intense teamwork keep most rowers in the sport for life. Many rowers compete at the world-class level for nine or ten years.

As collegiate rowing blossomed and spread across the country, it was faced with the challenge of instituting a

The New York Athletic Club's Larry Klecastsky, age 46, competing in the 1985 Head of the Charles in Boston. He represented the U.S. in lightweight doubles at the World Championships until the early 1980s, and continues to win medals at the extremely competitive Royal Canadian Henley Regatta. As of 1986, he had won 62 medals there, including 10 in the Senior 145-pound singles.

national championship. The Intercollegiate Rowing Championship (called IRA), established in 1895, was the first attempt to hold a championship. But its validity as a championship was weakened by the fact that Harvard and Yale usually did not attend because the race often fell on the same day as their traditional match against each other. The IRA location on the East Coast also discouraged the participation of top West Coast crews, who could not justify the expense of sending a team to Syracuse, New York.

The national championship issue was finally resolved in 1982 by Bill Engeman, a rower and lawyer in Cincinnati who organized the first Cincinnati Regatta. Engeman invited the best crew from the East (winner of the Eastern Sprints), the best crew from the West (winner of the Pacific Coast Championship), and the winner of the Harvard-Yale race to attend the fledgling regatta. He sealed his offer by volunteering to pay their way to Cincinnati. Engeman and his organizing committee worked a near miracle in transforming a newly created lake in East Fork State Park, with no rowing course, no facilities, and no equipment, into a championship site. Yale won the first Cincinnati Regatta, which was a success and which is now recognized as the National Collegiate Championship.

Rowing may have initiated intercollegiate athletics in this country, but it was actually professional rowing that spawned competitive American rowing. In the mid 1800s, professional watermen, who earned their living on the country's waterways, found that money could be made through rowing contests. The public, seeking activities to fill their increasing leisure time, quickly embraced the sport, as did the media, the promoters, and the gamblers. Ironically, rowers, who are rarely in the spotlight now, were national heroes in the 1850s. Men such as James Hamill, Edward Hanlan, and the Biglin brothers took anywhere from $50 to $3,000 a race for competing in fours, pairs, doubles, or singles. In 1879 Hanlan earned almost $12,000 in prize money, a princely sum in those days. Some rowing contests drew crowds of as many as 20,000 spectators.

As rowing became a big-time sport, it also became corrupt. Several scandals in the 1870s, including fixed races and other trickery such as sawing a shell in half, led to the decline of professional rowing and its virtual disappearance by the 1900s. Before its exit from the sporting scene, professional rowing led to the establishment of the organization that is now called USRowing. The organization was originally called the National Association of Amateur Oarsmen and was founded in 1872 to define the term "amateur" and thereby enable true amateurs to distinguish themselves from the tainted professionals. This distinction

enabled amateurs to compete separately without the influ-
ence of the professionals and their shady associates.

The NAAO was a membership organization for amateur
clubs that put on the national championships beginning in
1823. In 1929 the NAAO voted to include colleges and
individuals into its membership. In 1978 the NAAO's role
expanded with the ratification of the Amateur Sports Act.
The Sports Act was designed to clear up the muddled
amateur sports scene in America. Prior to 1978 the Amateur
Athletic Union (AAU), the United States Olympic Committee (USOC), and numerous sports organizations all exerted
undefined jurisdiction in governing amateur sports and in
selecting the U.S. Olympic teams. The Sports Act decreed
that each sport—rowing, track and field, etc.—would develop its own national governing body. The USOC was
given the role of handling all Olympic affairs in coopera-
tion with the national governing bodies. In 1981 the
growth of women's rowing instituted a name change in
which the NAAO became the United States Rowing Association or USRowing.

Today the USRA or USRowing is a nonprofit organization that promotes rowing nationwide and serves those who
row. USRowing sponsors six regional championships and
national championships for men, women, Juniors, and
Masters. USRowing also develops, selects, and funds teams
to represent the United States at the World Rowing Championships, World University Games, Pan Am Games, and
the Olympics. Currently, 40 percent of the USRowing
individual members are women. Until recently, the National Women's Rowing Association was the predominant
organization for women rowers. The NWRA used to sponsor the national championships for women, which are now
held by USRowing.

One of the pioneers in women's rowing was Ernestine
Bayer. In 1938 Bayer and 12 friends founded the Philadelphia Girls Rowing Club, which was the first women's
rowing club on Boathouse Row. Bayer, who is in her
seventies, continues to row and is the longstanding secre-

5

tary of the Alden Ocean Shell Association. The first women's club in the United States was ZLAC of San Diego, which was founded in 1892 by Zulette (Lamb) and Lena, Agnes, and Carolina (Polhamus).

Arthur Martin was another pioneer in rowing. In 1971 Martin designed a stable, durable shell that could be rowed in all kinds of conditions and cost under $1,000. Martin's stable, inexpensive (in comparison to a racing shell) boat, the Alden Ocean Shell, appealed to people who wanted to row for fun or fitness. Soon after the invention of the Alden Ocean Shell, an association was established to bring the Ocean Shell owners together. The Alden Ocean Shell Association has members across the country and is one of USRowing's largest registered clubs. The Association sponsors numerous competitions and even a national championship for Alden owners. The Alden Ocean Shell made rowing accessible to the weekend rower and was the pioneer in the recreational shell market, which has continued to expand as recreational rowing has become increasingly popular. Recreational rowers now benefit from a wide variety of recreational shells on the market and from a wide variety of rowing opportunities, such as open-water rowing. In open-water competition, competitors race 3–30 miles across open water, such as the ocean. These races test the rowers' watermanship and navigating skills, as well as their stamina and rowing ability.

A 95-year-old photograph that hangs in the Vesper boathouse. Only the Undine Barge Club (far left) remains essentially unchanged, while (left to right) the Penn Athletic Club, College Boat Club (U. Penn), Vesper Boat Club/Malta Boat Club, and University Barge Club have been significantly altered.

SWEEP ROWING

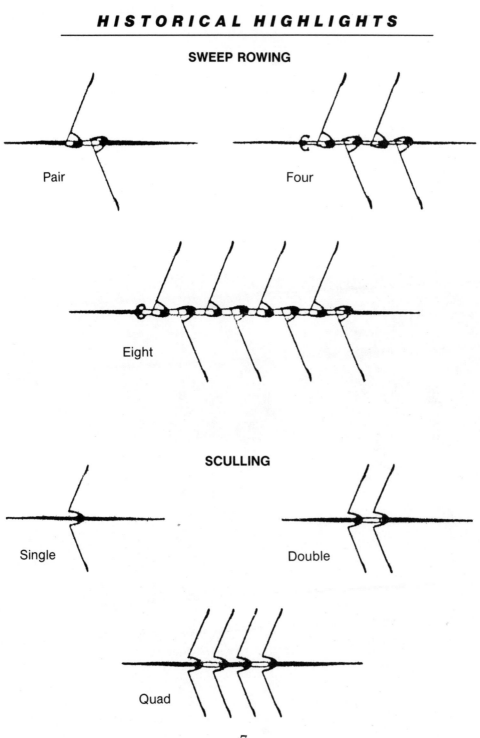

Pair

Four

Eight

SCULLING

Single

Double

Quad

Durham Boat Club, New Hampshire. Lightweight sculler Bob Dreher, 1983.

2
SCULLING TECHNIQUE

Rowing with two 9½-foot oars, or "sculls," is called sculling. Sculling is done in boats of one, two, or four people, which constitute a single, double, or quad. Technically, the term "rowing" applies specifically to sweep rowing, in which each rower handles one 12½-foot oar. Two, four, or eight people row in sweep boats, which are called a pair, four, or eight. Technicalities aside, the terms rowing and sculling will be used interchangeably throughout this book to describe the motion of propelling a single shell through the water.

Sculling is easy to learn. Doug Herland, a 1984 Olympian, has taught hundreds of people to row. Herland says that most people can row a single after only 15–30 minutes of instruction. However, *mastering* the technique provides a fascinating challenge. The quest for that perfect stroke that feels just right can hook you on the sport for life.

The best way to learn how to scull is to take lessons or attend a clinic where you can receive live instruction from experienced scullers. It's important to learn correct technique in the beginning. Taking lessons will allow you to observe and then to receive immediate coaching and feed-back as you try the skills yourself. Most clubs are eager to teach novices how to row, and they provide clinics or lessons for anyone who wants to learn. There is a list of USRowing clubs in the Appendix. If you don't have a club in your area, contact your parks and recreation department to see if they sponsor lessons. They often do if a rowable body of water is under their jurisdiction. Also, boat manu-facturers and dealers often give lessons or have a pro on staff who teaches sculling. Another way to learn is to attend a sculling camp. A week at camp in a scenic, secluded spot can double as a vacation. For instance, Craftsbury Sculling School is located in northeastern Vermont on a spring-fed lake that is also the town's water supply. Aspiring scullers receive daily instruction from visiting elite coaches and then hone their skills by touring the lake and watching for moose and elk along its wild, undeveloped shoreline. If you live in an area where rowing is not established, you may have to teach yourself to scull and take up the sport on your own. USRowing can provide information and resources that will help you get started.

Getting back to the business of learning to scull, it is helpful to have a clear image of the sculling stroke in your mind before you ever take to water. Studying pictures, descriptions, and videos of sculling will enable you to visualize correct technique and to understand coaching instructions. Before starting, it also helps to have a basic understanding of sculling terminology and equipment.

Sculling is a smooth, continuous motion in which one stroke flows into the next. An expert sculler makes the motion look effortless. He uses a quiet, powerful stroke that subtly propels the boat without checking its forward mo-mentum. Aspiring scullers have been known to watch films of Finland's graceful Pettri Karppinen and think they could beat him in their grandfather's wherry; but looks are deceiving. Karppinen has three Olympic gold medals and is currently one of the fastest scullers in the world in single sculls.

SCULLING TECHNIQUE

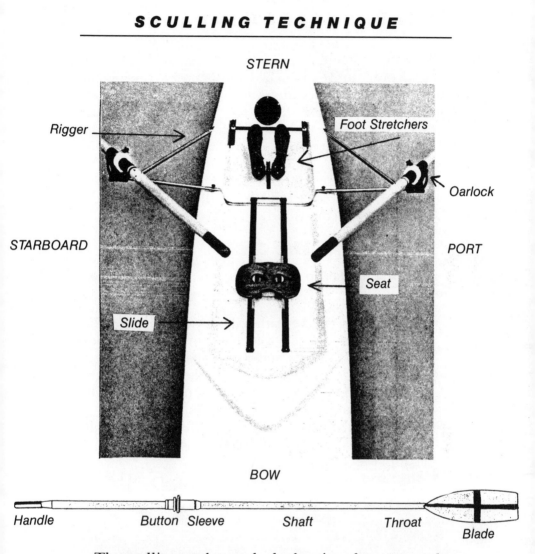

The sculling stroke can be broken into four stages: the catch, drive, finish or release, and recovery. The *catch* is the stage in which the oar blades enter ("catch") the water to begin the stroke. The catch is followed by the *drive*, in which the power of the legs, upper body, and arms is used to drive the oars through the water. The blade leaves the water at the end of the stroke, which is called the *finish*. The motion of releasing the blade from the water is called the *release*. After the finish, the body moves up the slide into the stern of the boat and prepares for the next catch. This rest time between strokes is called the *recovery*. During the recovery the oar blades are *feathered*; feathering the oars means to turn the blades flat as they travel through the air to decrease wind resistance. The blades are turned square, or *squared*, just before they enter the water again at the catch.

The following descriptions and photographs explain sculling in detail. Studying them will help you create a visual goal to work toward when you get on the water.

THE GRIP

Good sculling technique begins with a proper grip on the oars.

- With your oars in the feathered position and blades flat on the water, position your hand so that your index finger is flush with the end of the handle.
- Wrap your fingers loosely around the handle. A tight grip tires your forearms. There should be a straight line from your elbow to your knuckles.
- Place your thumb over the end of the oar and apply light pressure against it to keep the oar button pressed against the oarlock.
- The handle should never touch the palm of your hand.

The wrist is slightly broken as the handle is rolled out onto the fingers. The fingers don't actually shift their grip on the handle.

With the blade squared, the fingers reach all the way around the handle, the wrist is flat, and the thumb is on the end of the handle.

BLADEWORK

Use your fingers to do all bladework. Your wrist remains flat and only flexes as a result of your fingers' movement.

Feathering: Feathering the blade is turning it from square to flat to reduce wind resistance as the blade travels through the air during the recovery. The oar has squared edges where it fits against the oarlock so you can feel its shaft rotate and drop into position. To feather the blade, rotate the oar by rolling the handle forward with your fingers and then relax your grip to let the blade drop into the feathered position.

Squaring: Squaring the blade is turning it from flat (horizontal) to square (vertical) to "catch" the water and propel the boat. To square the blade, roll the handle back with your fingers and relax your grip to let the oar rotate into the squared position.

THE CATCH

The catch is the stage of the stroke in which the blades enter the water and begin the drive or pull-through.

- Coil yourself at the top of the slide so that your shins are nearly vertical. Press your torso against your thighs

13

and keep your knees under your armpits or between your arms, never outside your arms. Although you are leaning forward, you should be sitting tall, not slouched.

Preparation for the Catch. Here the sculler has completely squared his blades and is moving the last inches toward placement of the blades. His shins are nearly vertical. The stern of the single is buried in the water because most of the weight is on the foot stretchers. This is the most vulnerable part of the stroke, and care must be taken not to move the knees from side to side or drop one hand or the other, or the boat will upset or lurch to one side.

The Catch. The handles are lifted by a movement from the shoulder and the blades are quickly and directly dropped into the water. The shell's stem remains buried in the water, and the sculler's shins are vertical to the line of the wash box. His neck is relaxed, with full compression of the body being reached by bringing the torso in contact with the thighs. The thighs should be close to the calves. The arms are straight, but not locked, and the shoulder blades are fully extended with the arms.

- With arms straight, stretch forward and outward to obtain maximum reach.
- Keep your wrists flat so that a straight line can be drawn from your shoulder to your knuckles.
- Square your blades and submerge them so that the water just covers them.
- Keep your head up and your eyes forward.

THE DRIVE

The drive is the power portion of the stroke. Your legs, back, and arms each supply part of the force. For descriptive purposes, the drive is divided into segments according to which body part is doing most of the work at a particular point. However, all your muscles should coordinate their movements throughout the drive to provide a smooth, continuous application of power.

The Leg Drive. The strong drive with the legs accompanies a slight opening of the upper body. The shoulder blades transmit the power through the straightened arms. The weight is beginning to shift into the bow, so the stern is no longer buried in the water. Note the "lump" of water behind the blades as the boat is accelerated. A rower should try to have the sensation of stretching the shoulder blades out of the body, or of barely being able to hold onto the handles because of the leg drive.

The Back Drive. The oars are perpendicular to the boat as the upper body passes the vertical position. The legs are nearly flat as the arms start to pull to the body. Note the closeness of the hands to each other as the oar handles cross over, and the bend in the shaft of the near blade, indicating the amount of pressure being applied. The shell is running evenly from bow to stern. When the oars are perpendicular, the most efficient pressure is being applied. Also note that the rower checks his course (by turning his head) only when the oars are in the water and the boat is more stable than during the recovery.

Arm Pull to the Body. A forceful finish with the arms "sends" the boat for the recovery phase. The upper body is comfortably leaning into the bow, with its weight supported by the stomach muscles. There is not an excessive drop in the lower back, which would dump the momentum of the rower's body into the bow. The wrists are flat as the handles are drawn close to the rib cage. The handles are kept high enough so that the blades don't "wash out" or exit the water before the actual release. Here, the rower may have too much tension in his neck. The bow is riding lower in the water than in the previous photo.

During the drive, think of your hands as hooks and pull the oar back without squeezing it. Your oarlocks will be set so that your left oar is slightly higher than your right and your hands will just clear each other when you pull the oars toward your body.

The drive/legs: Seventy-five percent of the power of the sculling stroke is provided by your legs, which begin the drive.

- Drive against the stretchers with your legs.
- Do not change your upper-body position. Keep your arms straight and fully extended, with wrists flat. Keep your head up and eyes forward.
- Let your legs do all the work during this stage. Keep the rest of your body fixed to transmit the power of your legs to the oars efficiently.

The drive/back: When your legs are almost fully extended, your back takes over.

- Keep your legs nearly straight.
- Lean back or "swing" into the bow.
- Keep your arms straight and transmit the power of your back drive into the oars.
- Move your head and shoulders in a straight line. Your shoulders should be relaxed, not hunched.

The drive/arms:

- When your back has nearly completed its lean into the bow, bend your elbows and arms forcefully, and smoothly pull the handles into your body so that your thumbs almost touch the bottom of your rib cage.
- Your back should be firm and provide a base for your arms to pull from.

The drive is a smooth, continuous motion in which the movements of your legs, back, and arms overlap to provide constant power. Your legs start the drive; as they finish, your back takes over; as your back finishes, your arms begin their pull and complete the drive. Your body seems to "hang" on the oar and uses all its power to accelerate the oars through the stroke.

THE FINISH AND RELEASE

The finish is the point in the stroke at which the blades are released from the water.

The Release. At the release the handles follow a circular motion as the blades are lifted out of the water and feathered flat. The upper body has not changed position from the previous photo. The wrists are broken slightly as the oar handles are rolled out into the fingers. The bow rides low in the water as the boat accelerates. Elbows are kept close to the body. The sculler here seems not to have pushed his left handle down far enough, because his far blade is scraping the water.

- Make sure your legs are fully extended and pressed flat.
- Your stomach muscles should stop your upper body's swing into the bow. Your upper body should lean past vertical into the one o'clock position (viewed from the starboard side).
- With your wrists flat, pull the handles into the bottom of your rib cage and gently tap them down to release the blades from the water.

THE RECOVERY

The recovery is the motion in which you slide up to the stern to prepare for another catch.

- As you tap the oars out of the water at the finish, feather them and push them away from your body. Think of tapping the oars out and pushing the handles away as one "down and away" motion.

Beginning of Recovery. The upper body in its laid-back position as the arms straighten and the handles move away from the body. The boat moves fastest during this part of the stroke. The left (far) blade is still dragging, while the right blade is correctly off the water.

Crossover on Recovery. The hands cross each other closely as the body begins to swing from the hips into the stern. The arms are almost straight, and the knees begin to bend slightly as the rower pulls himself toward the foot stretchers with his toes.

19

Late Recovery. The rower's upper body has swung past vertical and the arms have completely straightened as he has come a quarter of the way up the slide. Shoulders continue to be low and relaxed, wrists flat, and the boat still runs on keel, equally weighted between bow and stern. The upper-body angle will not change between this point and until just after the catch.

Beginning of Square-Up. The rower has come two-thirds of the way up the slide as his wrists start to square the blades. The stern begins to sink, and the shins approach vertical. Now his right blade seems to be dragging on the water. His body angle is set for the catch.

- As you straighten your arms and move forward, and your hands pass over your knees, your body follows your arms and begins its forward lean while your legs are still flat.
- Your legs follow your body as your knees rise and your shins approach vertical.

- When your arms are straight and fully extended, square your oars so that they are ready to drop into the water at the catch. Square the oars well before the catch.
- Think of the recovery as a chain reaction toward the stern. Imagine a rope pulling your arms forward, then your upper body and finally your knees.
- Don't hurry the recovery or rush the slide. The recovery allows the boat to run out and utilize the momentum of the drive. The recovery should take almost twice as long as the drive. Rushing the slide jerks the boat backward and interrupts its run as your body weight shifts from bow to stern.
- Do not pull yourself up the slide with your feet. Let the momentum of your arms and upper body and the motion of the boat draw you forward.

COACHING TIPS

- Keep your shoulders down and relaxed. Do not hunch them.
- Make all your movements smooth, steady, and controlled. Any sudden movement of your body impedes the run of the boat. Lunging into the stern for the catch jerks the boat backward. Falling into the bow pushes the bow deeper into the water, increasing water resistance and decreasing speed.
- Only your blades should be buried. Do not lift the handles as you pull and thereby bury the oars deeply in the water. The blades should float; you simply pull. Let the oars float while you sit motionless and observe their position in the water.
- Make sure that your head and shoulders travel in a straight line. Your head weighs about fifteen pounds and can unbalance the boat when you move it off line.
- Keep your back firm. It provides a stable platform for your arms and legs to work from. Failing to set the lower back against the legs at the catch results in "shooting the tail," in which your rear slides back into

the bow without transferring any power into the oars. Sitting "tall" gives you more room in your lap to feather and enables your lungs to expand fully.

- Think of the oar handles as following a continuous elliptical path.
- Maintain a relaxed hold on the handles, keeping your wrists flat.
- Keep the blades as close to the water as possible so that they don't have far to drop at the catch. A long drop to the water upsets the balance of the boat.
- Relax and let your body swing into the stroke naturally.
- Keep your eyes looking ahead of you. Don't watch your oars; instead, feel what they are doing.
- Release and catch both blades simultaneously. Failing to do so results in different stroke lengths for each oar and causes the boat to veer from a straight course.
- Study the sculling stroke before you try it; this will help you learn the technique faster when you get on the water.

SAFETY

Before you take your first stroke on the water, keep some important safety considerations in mind.

- You must be able to swim. While wide, stable recreational shells make flipping over unlikely, it is still a possibility for which you need to be prepared. Being a good swimmer enables you to be comfortable and confident in the water.
- Know the first rule of boating safety, which is **always stay with the boat**. If the shell capsizes, it will provide sufficient flotation to support you even if it is full of water.
- The Coast Guard requires you to carry a life preserver in a recreational shell.
- Cold water and air temperature pose a serious threat to rowers. If you capsize in cold water, you run the risk of

hypothermia or death in severe conditions. When the water temperature is below 50° Fahrenheit and/or the air temperature is less than 40°F, a launch (motorboat) should be within 100 yards of your shell for rescue purposes. If you row in cold conditions, you should wear nonabsorbent, high-insulation clothing such as wool and polypropylene. A life jacket will provide additional insulation. If you capsize in cold water, try to get as much of your body as possible onto the shell and out of the water. If you can't get out of the water, draw your knees up to your chest and wrap your arms around them to help conserve body heat. Other cold-water precautions are to row near the shore and to use a buddy system. Anytime you go out alone, tell someone where you are going and when you plan to return.

- Waving your hands or a shirt in the air is a distress signal. For eights, raising one oar vertical to the boat is also a sign of distress.

- Know the traffic pattern on the water. When an official pattern exists, it is often posted in the boathouse. If nothing is posted, consult other users of the water, especially other rowers who will also be going backward. If no pattern is established, set one up. Motorboats are an irritant to rowers, but other shells are more dangerous.

- If your shell has quick-release shoes, check them every time you go out to be sure they will release your feet properly.

- For high visibility, wear white in the morning and evening. Wear bright colors during the day. Remember that you sit low in the water and are difficult to see.

- Be wary of rowing out a distance with a tail wind and then turning around and finding it too rough to row back.

- On hot days and long rows, be sure to drink fluids. Carry a water bottle.

- Inspect your equipment before taking it onto the water: Close all ports tightly. Make sure all hardware is tightened down—bolts should be snug but not too tight. Make sure the outriggers are fastened securely to the shell.

GETTING READY TO ROW: RIGGING THE BOAT

The shell's hardware, or rigging, should be adjusted, or "rigged," to fit you. A proper fit enables you to row correctly and comfortably. The beginning sculler should be concerned with three basic rigging adjustments. The first adjustment is the *foot stretcher position*. This adjustment should be made when you are sitting in the boat. With your legs straight, your stretchers should be moved either forward or backward so that when you pull the oar handles into your body, your thumbs, which are placed over the ends of the handles, just touch the bottom of your rib cage

The rower is sitting in the finish position, illustrating the closeness of the handles to the ribs and the height of the handles. In this case the handles may be a little too high.

when you're sitting upright. If you find yourself ramming into the front or back of your seat tracks, you need to adjust your foot stretchers accordingly. If the handles hit your body, move the stretchers toward the bow. If the handles swing wide of your body, move the stretchers closer to the stern.

The second adjustment is *oarlock height,* and it should also be determined when you are sitting in the boat. The left oarlock should be rigged one-half inch above the right to allow your hands to clear each other during the stroke. Both oarlocks should be set so that your thumbs on the handles just touch the bottom of your rib cage when you pull the handles into your body. If your oars are rigged too high, the blades will frequently miss water. If the oarlocks are too low, you will have trouble lifting the blades out of the water.

The third rigging adjustment is *pitch.* Pitch is the angle of the blade relative to the water when the oar is perpendicular to the boat and the blade is square in the water. The top edge of the blade should tilt slightly toward the stern of the boat. This slight tilt of five to seven degrees keeps the blade from driving too deep into the water when you pull back on the oars. You can gauge pitch adequately by simply looking at the blade when the oar is perpendicular to the boat. The top of the blade should tilt toward the stern. You can change the tilt of the blade by making an adjustment at the oarlock. Your owner's manual and or your dealer can advise you specifically on how to make the adjustment on your particular shell. Some rowers measure pitch more scientifically with an angle meter or rowing specific "Pitchmaster" tool. However, beginners will do well to concentrate on sculling technique and not worry too much about detailed rigging. Some instructors advise novices not to worry about pitch at all until they have mastered the stroke mechanics which will have more effect on their sculling than minor adjustments to pitch.

The importance of fine-tuning the rigging increases in proportion to the sculler's skill level. Additional adjustments that can increase a shell's speed by a few seconds are crucial to the elite-level sculler but insignificant to the beginner who is still trying to learn correct technique. As your skill level improves, you may want to study rigging further. It is a science that you can spend a lot of time experimenting with if you are mechanically inclined.

One other equipment adjustment that you should check is the position of the buttons on your oars. Set them so that your hands cross over each other when the oars are perpendicular to the boat. Compare your oars to be sure that the buttons are set at the same place on both oars. Buttons are set once and then forgotten.

The method you use to adjust stretcher position and oarlock height depends on the type of shell you have. Your owner's manual should tell you exactly how to make rigging adjustments. Anyone who sells you a boat should show you how to rig your boat and should be willing to rig it for you.

CARRYING YOUR SHELL

A good point to remember with regard to carrying your shell to water is that the workout is supposed to be rowing, not carrying the boat. One way to conserve energy for rowing is to find someone to help you carry your shell. A recreational shell can be easily carried by two people, with one person at the bow and one at the stern. If no help is available, you will have to analyze your strength and your equipment to decide how to carry the forty-to-fifty-pound boat. Some people carry the boat on one shoulder or at their hip, while others have sufficient strength and coordination to balance the boat on top of their heads and steady it with the riggers as they walk. Before trying this method on your own, practice it with someone around to help steady the boat while you learn to balance it. Some recreational shells have drop-in rigging, which can be removed from the cockpit and carried separately. The shell is a lot more wieldy with the riggers removed. The shell is even more manageable if you purchase or make a cart on which you can wheel your shell to the water. The main thing to remember when carrying your shell is to stay within your physical limits so that you don't hurt yourself or damage the boat.

Some attention should also be given to carrying the oars. Carry your oars blade first with the concave side up to reduce the chance of damage if the blades bump into something. The oars should also be laid down with the concave side of the blade up. If stepped on, the blades are less likely to break in this position.

GETTING IN AND PUSHING OFF

Once your equipment is safely to the water, you are ready to get in.

- Make sure the boat is parallel to the dock.
- Place the near-side oar into the oarlock and fasten the keeper. Many oars will only fit into the lock at the throat (near the blade).
- Lay the other oar in the outside oarlock and slide it out so that the button presses against the oarlock. Fasten the oarlock before you get in, and make sure the oar is perpendicular to the boat with the blade flat in the water. This balances the boat.
- Loosen the laces or Velcro straps of the shoes or foot stretchers.
- Push the seat toward the bow into the position where you will want to sit in it. The opening in the seat should face the bow.
- Hold both oar handles with your outside hand. Remember to *never let go of your oars*. The oars balance the boat as long as you are holding them. Hold onto the dock and near-side rigger with your inside hand.
- Place your outside foot onto the footboard between the seat rails. In most recreational shells you can step anywhere in the bottom of the boat without damaging the hull; however, in a racing shell, stepping anywhere but the footboard will put a hole in the bottom of the

While gripping the gunwale with one hand and holding the oar handles with the other, lower yourself onto the seat.

Fasten the stretchers.

Move the seat toward the stern and reach out with the right oar, keeping the left oar flat.

boat. It's good to get into the habit of stepping only where the manufacturer has intended.

- Transfer your weight into the boat and sit down. For the sake of balance, it is important that you put your foot down before you transfer your weight.
- Place your feet in the stretchers. Fasten the stretchers, but leave the straps or laces loose enough so that you can free your feet quickly if you capsize. If your boat has built-in shoes, make sure that the heels are attached to the foot stretchers so that you can pull your feet out without using your hands.
- Push away from the dock with your inside hand and lean out slightly to raise the inside oar and prevent it from scraping across the dock.

LEARNING TO SCULL

Plan to spend your first several outings getting the feel of your boat and learning correct technique. Vincent Ventura, men's sculling coach at the New York Athletic Club, advises

29

beginners to take their time and not to try to apply power too soon. Resist the temptation to row full force until you have learned to scull correctly and can use your energy effectively.

Fred Borchelt, a 1984 Olympic silver medalist, recommends the following learning sequence for beginners:

- Have someone hold the stern of your boat at the dock so that you can practice handling the oars from a stationary position.
- Practice the "safe" position. Straighten your legs and hold both oars perpendicular to the boat with the blades flat on the water. This is called the safe position because the boat is virtually untippable as long as you hold onto both oars. Assume the safe position whenever you need to steady the boat.

This is the "safe" position, with both oars perpendicular to the shell, blades flat, hands touching. Keep this position when a motorboat wake or wind makes your boat unsteady.

- Alternately lift one blade off the water and then the other to feel how the motion affects the boat's balance.

- Practice squaring one oar while leaving the other blade flat on the water. Practice squaring the other oar.
- Square one blade and practice putting it in and out of the water; leave the other blade flat on the water. Practice with the other blade.
- Brush one oar back and forth across the water, then do the same with the other.
- Practice complete strokes with one blade and without using the slide. Square the blade, drop it into the water, pull it through the water, lift it out, and feather it.
- Practice complete strokes with both blades and no slide.
- After rowing for a while with arms only, add upper-body swing and bend from the waist as you take your strokes. Add the slide portion of the stroke gradually. Start by coming up half of the slide, increase to using three-quarters of the slide, and finally add the full slide so that you begin each stroke coiled in the catch position. This gradual progression from paddling (using your arms only) to using the full slide also makes an excellent warm-up drill.

Here are some additional coaching tips:

- Harry Parker, head crew coach at Harvard University, advises beginners to concentrate on coordinating the use of the legs and back to apply force evenly. He recommends practicing with just the arms, and then gradually adding the upper body and slide to develop a long, full stroke.
- Tony Johnson, head crew coach at Yale University, emphasizes that beginners need to relax in the boat. He suggests that you row without using the slide until you have practiced bladework and feel comfortable with the boat's balance. He reminds beginners not to squeeze the oar and to pull on it through the entire length of the stroke. The top of the blade should be covered by the water.
- Vincent Ventura recommends rowing with the blades

square (not feathering them) to practice balancing the boat. This technique also helps you practice catches and a proper finish and release from the water.

- Larry Gluckman, head crew coach at Princeton University, suggests you have someone watch you practice and critique your stroke. Ideally you should have someone videotape you so that both you and a coach can analyze your stroke.

BOAT-HANDLING SKILLS

During your first outing, you should also practice basic boat-handling skills, which are essential to your safety, comfort, and confidence on the water.

Stopping: To stop the momentum of the boat, all you have to do is square the blades in the water and "hold water."

To stop the boat, or "check it down" or "hold water," turn the blades vertically in the water.

Backing: Backing is done to move the boat toward the stern. Think of it as the reverse of a normal stroke. Square the blades so that the concave side faces the bow. Insert the blades in the water up by the stern (where you would normally be releasing them from the water). Push forward on the handles to propel the boat toward the stern.

Turning: You can make a gradual turn by taking longer strokes with one oar. You can make a sharper turn by holding one blade square in the water and sculling with the other. To pivot the boat on its axis, scull with one oar and back with the other.

Steering: Maintain a straight course by looking at a landmark in front of you (off the stern) and aligning the stern and the wake of the boat with that landmark. If you start to get out of alignment, you can make slight adjustments by taking a longer stroke with the appropriate oar.

Rowing with the right oar as the left oar returns.

Backing with the left oar as the right oar returns.

You should periodically look around to make sure your path is clear of rocks, stumps, boats, and other hazards. To check your course while you're rowing, turn your head only and do it during the drive, when the blades are buried and will stabilize the boat. If you find yourself drifting off course, you may be taking longer strokes with one oar or you may be releasing one blade from the water sooner than the other. Concentrate on catching and releasing the blades simultaneously, and on taking the same stroke length with each oar.

You should also know how to handle these situations:

Catching a crab: Catching a crab is the expression used when your oar gets stuck in the water and you can't release it. The primary causes are placing the oar in the water before it's squared and feathering the oar before it's out of the water. The trapped oar pulls you toward the water, and a big crab can pull the boat over. To recover from a crab, stop sculling with the other oar and lean toward it to shift the boat and lift the trapped oar from the water.

Capsizing: Tipping over is common in rowing. Even elite scullers flip over occasionally. If your boat tips, try to relax your body and slide out of the boat as gently as possible to avoid damaging the shell. Always stay with the boat. If the water is cold, get back in or at least on top of the boat. Swim with the boat to shallow water where you can dump the water out and get back in easily. If the bulkheads are full of water, lift the boat slowly to empty the water. If you lift the boat quickly, the weight at the bow and stern may cause the boat to break.

DOCKING

When your practice is over, you are ready to dock and disembark. Point the bow at a thirty-degree angle toward the dock. Coast in, and when your bow is nearly to the dock, square your outside blade and lean out. That will turn the boat parallel to the dock. It will also help you raise your inside oar off the dock.

To get out of the boat, position the oars perpendicular to

Start to drag the outside oar as you approach the dock to turn the shell parallel to the dock.

Place both handles in your outside hand as the boat slides parallel to the dock. Grab the dock with the inside hand while the outside hand holds both handles.

the boat, with the outside blade flat on the water. Hold both oars with your outside hand and hold onto the inside rigger and the dock with your inside hand. Place your outside foot on the footboard and lift your weight until you can step onto the dock with your inside foot. Place your foot on the dock before you transfer your weight to it. Pull the outside oar in, take it out of the oarlock, and close the gate; then remove the inside oar, closing its gate too. Leaving oarlocks open is a good way to snap the gate off or scratch another boat in a crowded boathouse. If you row on saltwater, rinse the boat and oars, especially the metal parts, after every row. Wipe the shell down with a clean towel. When your boat gets dirty, wash it with mild soap. A polycoat auto wax every few months will restore a plastic boat's shine; a wooden boat will appreciate a coat of lemon oil.

DRILLS by Peggy O'Neal

The goal of doing a drill is to isolate parts of the stroke and try to make improvements. It is counterproductive to spend time doing a drill incorrectly or mindlessly. Therefore, have a specific goal in mind, do the drill for a specific period, and then move on.

ROWING WITH BLADES SQUARE

This is one of the most useful drills. Try doing long, steady pieces with the blades square.

Catch: By not having to feather the oars, you can concentrate on inserting the blade as you reach the front of your slide. When you add the feather, the timing of your catch should remain unchanged.

Release: Isolate the release from the feather. If you can get a clean release with no feather, you know you are dropping your hands properly to get the oars out of the water.

Recovery: Because your squared blades will catch unpleasantly if they hit the water, your balance will improve.

PAUSE DRILLS

Pause drills are used to practice relaxation, balance, and slide control during the recovery phase of the stroke. You should be relaxed and the boat should be balanced throughout the recovery. Your body should follow the correct sequence during the recovery in which your hands lead away toward 'the stern and your upper body and knees follow in a smooth, controlled chain reaction into the stern. Pause two to three seconds in each specified position while balancing the boat with the oars off the water and then continue the stroke.

Hands away: This is the first stage of the recovery. Finish the previous stroke, release the blades from the water. Move your hands away from your body (toward the stern) and pause. You should be relaxed and the boat should be balanced. Your upper body should be vertical and your legs should be flat in the boat.

Hands and upper body: After your hands move away, your upper body leans forward just past vertical (your knees stay flat in the boat). Pause at this point.

Half slide: Continue the recovery until you are halfway up the slide. Pause here. Your upper body should be completely ready for the catch—leaning forward, arms fully extended. Your forward lean should be completed. When you finish the slide, your fingers roll the blade square and your arms rotate from the shoulders to drop the blades into the water. Avoid rushing the last half of the slide and lunging forward. Your upper body angle should not change during the last half of the slide.

EYES CLOSED

For this drill you should either be accompanied by a launch or a buddy, or only row 10–20 strokes after a careful look around. Concentrate on relaxing, smoothness, and rhythm.

CONCENTRATION

Concentrate on specific parts of the stroke (catch, finish) for 20 strokes at a time.

AIR STROKES

Take three normal strokes, then pull through the next stroke with your blades square and just above the water. Good for balance.

HARD STROKES/PERFECT STROKES

Take three strokes that are as perfect as you can make them—relaxed, long, balanced, clean, etc. Then take three strokes at full pressure. Repeat. Try to notice the differences. Are you rushing up the slide? Blades getting caught? Shoulder or neck tensing up? Shortening your slide? Hanging on to the oars with a death grip?

VARIABLE SLIDES

The purpose of this drill is to practice body control, slide control, and the timing of the catch. Do 10 strokes using the full slide, 10 using three-quarters of the slide, 10 using half the slide, 10 using one-quarter of the slide, and 10 using arms and upper body only (no slide), and 10 using only arms (no upper body lean and no slide). Then add upper body swing and advance to using the full slide again in increments of ten strokes. Then repeat the original sequence using arms only. Remember, the goal is to extend your arms fully and drop the blades into the water for the catch at your full reach, whether you are using a full slide or no slide.

FULL PRESSURE AT FEWER THAN 10 STROKES PER MINUTE

See how far your boat will run between strokes.

Drills should be part of every warm-up. They will help focus your mind on your boat and body, as well as help you warm up physically. You can also spend an entire workout doing drills to improve your technique (perhaps after a hard workout).

Sample Warm-up (15 minutes)

- Hands only—1 minute
- Hands and back—1 minute
- ¼, ½, ¾, full slide—1 minute each
- ½ pressure—30 strokes
- Blades square—20 strokes

- ½ pressure—20 strokes; ¾ pressure—30 strokes
- Pause Drill—30 strokes (hands away, 10; hands and back away, 10; ½ slide, 10)
- ½ pressure—10 strokes; ¾ pressure—30 strokes; full pressure—30 strokes
- Catch Drill—10 strokes (Get a quick catch at maximum stretch. At half slide have maximum forward body angle and arms fully extended. As slide rolls toward catch, roll blades square. As slide reaches end, pivot arms from the shoulders, letting blades drop quickly into the water. As soon as blades are buried—not before!—legs start the drive.)
- Balance/recovery—10 strokes (Smooth release, oars come cleanly out of water and never bounce on surface; body totally relaxed—arms, neck, face, shoulders, legs, feet.)
- Work on a smooth acceleration from catch to finish.

Workout (30 minutes)

Cool-down (10 minutes)

- Eyes shut—1 minute (relax!)
- Feet out of foot stretchers—2 minutes
- Blades square—2 minutes
- Work on a perfect recovery—2 minutes
- Paddle easily—3 minutes

Trimline 19.

3
SHELLS AND EQUIPMENT

Twenty years ago rowing shells were designed with only the competitive sculler in mind. Boat builders handcrafted their sleek, delicate shells with the sole purpose of making them go faster than competitors' models in a 2,000-meter race. The price tag on those thoroughbred shells narrowed the consumer market to those who were serious competitors and were willing to pay for speed. Scullers who just wanted a good workout or a refreshing row around the lake had to settle for paddling about in wide, flat-bottomed rowboats.

Boat builders still handcraft racing shells that are in high demand by increasing numbers of competitive rowers. However, the fitness boom and the introduction of a versatile, moderately priced recreational shell opened a whole new market that now makes owning a shell feasible for scullers at all levels. Today, scullers can choose from a variety of shells designed to accommodate a wide range of uses, and priced at about $1,500.

When you decide to buy a shell, the first thing to consider is what you want to use it for. You will look for different specifications, depending on whether you plan to scull for

41

exercise, to fish, to go on camping tours, to row on open water, or to race with other recreational rowers at 2,000 meters or compete in long-distance, open-water events.

The second factor you should consider is where you plan to row. If you are going to encounter sizable waves on open water (either from wind or power boats), your boat will need a different design and features than one used to skim across a placid, sheltered lake.

A third consideration is how many people are going to use the shell. If your whole family is going to row regularly, you will need a shell that can be easily adjusted to fit each family member. You should also think about whether you're more interested in solo rowing or rowing with a

River Shell Single.

partner. Most manufacturers produce recreational doubles, and some of these boats can be converted into singles. Some singles also have space for carrying a passenger.

Seashell Single.

Another point to consider is where you will be storing your shell. A boathouse will easily accommodate a 24-foot shell, while your garage might not. It's a good idea to measure your storage facility before you buy. If the shell is not going to enjoy the protection of indoor storage, durability becomes a priority. Some shells are equipped with drop-in rigging that can be easily stored indoors, leaving only the hull to brave the elements. Drop-in rigging also makes transporting a shell easier by reducing the width and weight that must be managed in one trip. The dimensions of the shell will also determine whether it will fit on top of your car or require a trailer. Most single shells weigh between 30 and 50 pounds and can be car-topped without any problem.

The spectrum of boats on the market ranges from wherrys and skiffs, to short, flat-bottomed recreational shells, to longer, speedier recreational racers, to pure racing shells. Once you have analyzed your rowing needs and goals, the specifications of the various boats will tell you whether or not they are likely to meet your requirements.

The *width* of a shell largely determines how stable the

boat will be at the expense of speed. Dories, skiffs, and other wide, "rowboat"-type craft provide maximum stability, which would be desirable for fishing and taking passengers, especially children, for a ride. However, the beamy boats' lack of speed would quickly frustrate aspiring scullers eager to see and feel the results of their energy and improving technique in terms of speed and performance. On the other hand, racing shells are only 12 inches wide and deliver maximum speed relative to effort. However, their tendency to capsize at the hands of inexperienced beginners may dampen the novice's enthusiasm for the sport. Recreational shells fall between these extremes. The wider shells have a beam of about 28 inches, while rec-racer beams narrow to 20 inches or less.

Other factors that determine a boat's stability are the hull shape and the seat height. A flat hull and low seat lend more stability than a round hull and high seat. In deciding how stable your boat needs to be, analyze who will be using the boat and how they will row it. If you want to use your shell to exercise and also to fish, you will want a fairly stable recreational model that will tolerate some moving about by the occupant. If elite level competition is your ultimate

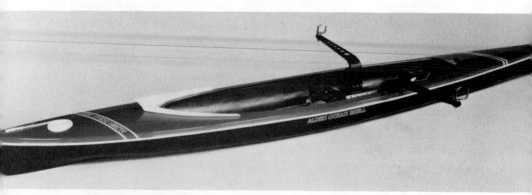

Alden Ocean Shell.

goal, you are better off taking lessons, learning to scull, and then buying a racing shell. The cost of shells makes buying a "beginner's" boat impractical if ultimately you plan to race seriously. Whatever your sculling goals, buy a shell that is stable enough for you to feel comfortable on the water. Comfort is essential for you to learn sculling technique and to enjoy spending time in the boat.

The shell's *length* affects its speed. Long shells knife through the water faster than short ones because their length absorbs the back-and-forth movement of the rower sliding along the tracks. Short shells tend to bounce up and down in the water as the rower's weight shifts fore and aft. Conversely, short shells can ride over waves and handle rougher conditions than 25-foot racing shells that are intended only for smooth water. Recreational shells are about 20 feet long, with the rec-racer types being longer.

Boston Rowing Shell.

The length of the boat will also determine where you can store it and how you transport it. A 25-foot shell may not fit in your garage, and it may be too long for your car or too unwieldy for you to carry.

The *weight* of the shell also affects how easily it can be transported. Most recreational shells weigh about 50–55 pounds fully rigged. Shells that come with drop-in rigging weigh about 40 pounds without the rigging, and the rigging assembly weighs about 20 pounds. Weight also affects the speed of the boat. A 30-pound racing single skims over the water much faster than a 60-pound shell.

When you begin shopping you should also be aware of the different materials boats are made of. If the shell will be rowed in rough conditions and used by a lot of people, you'll need a rugged hull that can withstand occasional bumps, collisions, and rough landings. Under this type of use, you'll also want the floor of the boat to tolerate being stepped on at any point. The bottom of a racing shell is only one-eighth to three-eighths inches thick, and stepping anywhere but the footboard will put a hole in the hull.

Outside storage necessitates durable, weather-resistant materials. Outdoors, a fiberglass hull will fare better than a wood one. Rigging and other exposed metal should be rust resistant. Drop-in rigging has the advantage of being easily stored indoors. In assessing the shell's durability, you should also examine the stress points where the riggers are attached to the hull to see if there is any reinforcement.

Adjustability is the next feature to consider. You should at least be able to adjust the height and pitch of the oarlocks and the position of the foot stretchers. Some shells allow you to make other rigging adjustments as well. The ease of adjusting the rigging will be important if several people will be using the boat and it will require frequent adjustments. If you are going to have to remove rigging to transport or store the shell, you should determine how easily the rigging can be detached. Quick-release pins or wing nuts are a plus if you have to adjust or remove the rigging frequently.

Depending on how you plan to use your boat, you may want to look into additional features. If you plan to carry equipment such as fishing or camping gear or a camera, you will want your shell to have storage space. Some open-water boats have splashboards and high coaming to help keep water out of the cockpit, while others have self-bailers to remove water from the cockpit after it gets in. If you like company when you row, consider a shell that will allow you to carry a passenger or that can convert into a double shell. Convertible boats should have a movable rowing station that can be centered for one person to row.

River Shell, double rigged as a single.

Seashell Double, Little River Marine.

Once you know what kind of shell you're looking for, send for information from various manufacturers. There is a list of dealers and manufacturers at the end of this chapter, and USRowing and *Small Boat Journal* publish an annual directory of builders, boats, equipment, and accessories. Studying the specifications of various boats will help you narrow your prospects down. After you have familiarized yourself with several models, talk to people who do the kind of rowing you plan to do and ask what kind of shell they would recommend and how their shell has performed. They may even be willing to let you try out their shell. The manufacturers or dealers should be willing to let you test-row their shells, so plan to try several models before you make a decision. Many manufacturers also give lessons or sponsor clinics that enable you to learn how to row while trying out their shells. Trade shows are also a good place to shop for shells.

Your shell should come with an owner's manual, which will explain how to rig and care for your particular model. Many owners' manuals also include sculling instructions. Your dealer should show you how to rig your boat and be willing to rig it for you. Some shells will come with oars that cost about $200–$300 if purchased separately. Oars are made out of either wood or carbon fiber. The main difference is that the carbon-fiber oars tend to be lighter and more durable.

Other accessories you may want to buy are a seat pad and a strokemeter. A seat pad cushions the hard wooden seat and makes the miles more comfortable. A strokemeter is a helpful training aid once you have become comfortable with sculling technique. It displays stroke rate, stroke count, and time. Many boat manufacturers and dealers publish a catalog of accessories.

Before you take the plunge and buy a shell, you may also want to look into the option of buying a rigging assembly that can convert a canoe, sailboard, or homemade boat into a rowable craft. Several companies manufacture drop-in rigging that can be adjusted to fit a variety of boats. This

Neilsen-Kellerman Strokecoach.

Alden Oarmaster, drop-in rigging.

option is worth looking into for someone who does a lot of canoeing or windsurfing, but would also like to do some rowing for fitness benefits. Drop-in rigging assemblies cost about $400. Some assemblies can also be converted into a rowing machine for indoor training.

You can take cost cutting a step further by building your own boat. Some boat manufacturers sell boat plans, and *The Small Boat Journal* is another source for these plans. Another cost-cutting option is to buy a used shell. When inspecting a used boat, you should make sure that the hull is smooth, that there are no cracks where the riggers attach to the hull, and that the joint that attaches the hull to the deck is sealed securely. *American Rowing* magazine and *USRowing News* publish classified ads that feature used equipment.

After you've bought a boat, you'll want to protect your investment with insurance. Author Julian Wolf, in his article "Insuring Your Shell" (*American Rowing*, Feb/Mar 1985), recommends that your coverage should include a comprehensive perils policy and personal liability insurance. The comprehensive perils policy will cover typical losses, such as collisions on the water, fire damage, theft, and transportation accidents. Your oars are not necessarily covered by your shell policy and may need to be insured separately. Personal liability insurance will cover you against damages or lawsuits that may be brought against you if you injure someone or damage property. Make sure you are covered for racing. Your insurance agent should be able to provide the additional coverage for your shell; however, you may also want to talk to agents who row and are experienced in insuring rowing equipment. USRowing can provide you with a list of agents who are familiar with rowing.

The New York Athletic Club's Jim Dietz, rowing legend, competing in the 1985 Head of the Charles in Boston. He now is the head crew coach at the U.S. Coast Guard Academy in New London, Connecticut.

SHELL MANUFACTURERS

Martin Marine Company, Inc., Box 251, Goodwin Rd., Kittery Point, ME 03905, (207) 439-1507

Advance USA, P.O. Box 452, East Haddam, CT 06423, (203) 873-8643

Laser International, P.O. Box 569, 1250 Tessier St., Hawkesbury, Ontario, Canada K6A 3C8, (613) 632-1181

R. E. Graham Corp., Rt. 2, 2351 Hwy. 28, Quincy, WA 98848, (509) 787-1225

Little River Marine, P.O. Box 986, Gainesville, FL 32602, (904) 378-5025

Small Craft, Inc., P.O. Box 766, Baltic, CT 06330, (203) 822-8269

Coffey Racing Shells, 48 East Fifth St., Corning, NY 14830, (607) 962-1982

Durham Boat Company, RFD #2, Newmarket Rd., Durham, NH 03824, (603) 659-2548

Easy Rider, P.O. Box 88108, Seattle, WA 98188, (206) 228-3633

Empacher, 4068 Ridge Ave., Philadelphia, PA 19129, (215) 849-3131

King Boat Works, P.O. Box 273, South Woodstock, VT 05071, (802) 457-1075

Bill Knecht, P.O. Box 1346, Camden, NJ 08105, (609) 966-3636

Maas Boat Co., 2100 Clement Ave., Alameda, CA 94501, (415) 865-5894

Omni-Cat Designs, 715 Emory Valley Rd., Oak Ridge, TN 37830, (615) 483-4387

Peinert Boatworks, 52 Coffin Ave., New Bedford, MA 02746, (617) 990-0105

George Pocock Racing Shells, Inc., 509 NE Northlake Way, Seattle, WA 98105, (206) 633-1038

Schoenbrod Racing Shells, 596 Elm St., Biddeford, ME 04005, (207) 283-3026

Vespoli USA, Inc., 385 Clinton Ave., New Haven, CT 06513, (203) 773-0311

DROP-IN RIGGING MANUFACTURERS

Durham Boat Company

R. E. Graham (EZ Rigger)

Martin Marine (Oarmaster)

Onboard Products (Onboard & Onboard II), 459 Main St., Amesbury, MA 01913, (617) 388-0162

Piantedosi Oars (RoWing), P.O. Box 643, West Acton, MA 01720, (617) 263-1814

Two Wesleyan University students, Alex Fowler (left) and Harry Berman doing a rowing machine test while cox Jaimé Tomé takes times.

4
ROWING MACHINES

As people become more health conscious and look for new ways to get in better shape, many are discovering the rowing machine as the perfect vehicle to fitness. Rowing uses all of the major muscle groups and provides a superb cardiovascular workout while toning and strengthening arms, legs, stomach, and back. The rowing machine enables you to enjoy a total workout in the comfort of your home, year-round.

Rowing machines are classified according to how they produce the resistance that provides the workout. The most common forms of resistance are hydraulic cylinders and fanned flywheels. You've probably seen the hydraulic types in your local sports store or fitness club. They have one or two arms that are each equipped with a shock absorber type of cylinder. The padded seat slides up and down on one or two rails on ball-bearing wheels. The rower straps his feet into the foot rests and uses the strength of his legs, arms, and upper body to pull the handles up from the floor and back toward him. The rower adjusts the machine's resistance by changing the angle of leverage on the rods of the hydraulic cylinders. Typical dimensions for these machines are 10 inches high, 30 inches wide, and 50 inches long. They weigh about 40 pounds and cost from $300 to $600, depending on the features they include. Some models come with electronic equipment that displays workout information such as time, speed, distance, number of strokes per minute, and calories burned.

Hydraulic machines are popular for several reasons. They are compact and can be stored on end to conserve space. They are relatively quiet, allowing you to work out while watching TV. Some of them enable you to isolate certain muscles and do strengthening exercises similar to weight lifting. Price is another reason people buy the hydraulic machines. You can get a hydraulic model for $300, while a flywheel model costs at least $600.

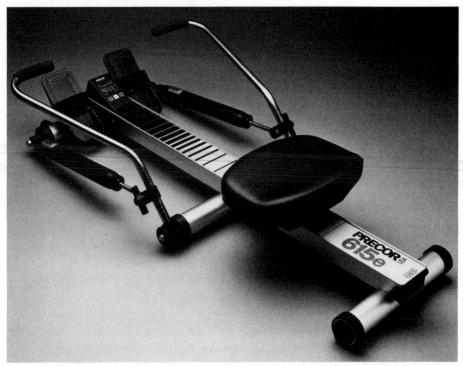

Precor 615E. (Photo courtesy of Precor)

Rowers are willing to pay more for a flywheel model because it more accurately simulates the motion of rowing a shell, whereas a hydraulic machine does not. The hydraulic machine may also fail to deliver a thorough workout at light resistance settings. If set at a load that's too light, some machines don't provide any resistance at all until you are well into the pull of your stroke. Consequently, the legs, which supply the power during the first part of the stroke, don't have to do much work.

The first popular flywheel rowing machine was invented in 1981 by competitive rowers for competitive rowers. Peter and Dick Dreissigacker built their original Concept II Rowing Ergometer in their barn, with the goal of producing an off-water training device for rowers. The Dreissigackers concede that many of their machines are now owned by people who don't race and have never rowed on water. The popularity of the flywheel design inspired at least three other companies to manufacture flywheel rowing machines.

The flywheel machines feature a sliding seat, foot straps, a flywheel of some sort, and a single handle that connects to the drive chain or cord that spins the wheel. When you pull the handle, your hands travel in the straight line pattern typical of rowing. True to rowing on water, the resistance increases as you pull harder and spin the wheel faster. The drive chain supplies smooth, continuous resistance that ensures a good workout.

Authenticity does have a few disadvantages, however. Most of the flywheel machines take up more room both to use and to store, and they tend to be noisy. If noise and storage space aren't a problem and you want the feel of real rowing, choose a flywheel machine. On the other hand, if you just want a workout, the hydraulic models are worth considering.

When you shop for a rowing machine, keep several points in mind. The most important is fit. The frame should be long enough so that you can stretch your legs out flat when you sit on it. The seat should not bump into the back edge of the rails when your legs are fully extended. The frame should not flex or lift off the ground when you row. If you are particularly strong, you will want to select a heavier frame.

Another important consideration is seat movement. The seat should roll smoothly, with minimum noise. Ball-bearing wheels tend to hold up the best, and the more wheels the better. Some models have an enclosed seat track, which provides extra protection from dents and dirt. Comfort is another feature you should consider. The seat should be well padded, water resistant, and durable. Likewise, the foot straps should be durable and comfortable. The frame should be rust resistant. Pivoting foot plates reduce strain on the ankles and calf muscles.

Pro Form Regatta. (Photo courtesy of Pro Form)

Test the machine thoroughly and analyze its performance. The tension should be easy to measure so that you can mark your progress, and the tension should also be easy to adjust when you sit on the machine. Resistance should be constant and continuous throughout the stroke at various speeds. The resistance cylinders should provide smooth, quiet tension; large cylinders tend to be more efficient and durable than small ones.

Your workouts will get monotonous if you don't have any way to measure your work rate and gauge performance. A strokemeter or stroke counter will make your workouts more interesting, as will an odometer. These features generally cost more but will be worth it if they keep you interested. If you want to do more than row on your machine, check to see if it has a seat lock. A seat lock will hold the seat in place so that you can isolate the upper body and do specific exercises to strengthen your arm, back, and chest muscles.

The important thing to remember is to start slowly and increase your work load gradually as your body adapts to the exercise. Your first few workouts should be rowed at light resistance so that you don't pull or strain a muscle. As your strength increases, you can set the resistance higher. Rowing slowly at high resistance builds strength, while rowing quickly at lighter resistance improves the cardiovascular system.

We've included some rowing machine workouts you might want to incorporate into your training program. Before you begin your workout schedule, you should read Chapter 5 on workouts, which discusses heart rate, aerobic and anaerobic exercise, stretching, and other important training principles. Before you row hard, learn to row right. Spend your first few workouts practicing good technique. Review the technique instructions in Chapter 2 and keep the coaching tips in mind. Rowing on a machine will not duplicate rowing in a shell exactly; however, general principles such as relaxation and coordination of legs, arms, and back apply to any type of rowing.

WORKOUT TERMINOLOGY

Ergometer: An exercise machine which measures your effort. For example, a rowing machine equipped with readout on speed or distance is an ergometer. Likewise a stationary bicycle qualifies as an ergometer if it can measure speed or distance. In this section, the term ergometer refers to the rowing machine.

Paddle: A term used by coaches and coxswains that means to row lightly using only your hands (no slide or body lean).

Piece: A segment of work.

Power ten: To take ten strokes at full pressure (all-out effort). Likewise, power twenty means 20 strokes of the same.

Pressure rating: The degree of force you apply to the oars. For instance, full pressure means to row as hard as you can. Three quarters pressure is ¾ of your full force and so forth down to one quarter pressure.

Steady state: A steady-state workout is exercising at a pace that doesn't leave you out of breath and that you can maintain for at least 30 minutes. You should be able to carry on a conversation with someone during a steady state workout.

Stroke rating: The number of strokes taken per minute.

WORKOUTS

The following workouts were designed and recommended by Concept II, Inc. Remember to warm up with light rowing and stretching before each workout, and to cool down with the same after the workout.

- For cardiovascular improvement, row at least 20 minutes at 70 percent of your maximum heart rate. Start the workout slowly and increase your speed gradually. Challenge yourself by trying to increase the distance you can row in 20 minutes.
- To practice for a 5-mile ergometer piece, row hard for one mile, then row easily for 3 minutes. Do 5 repetitions.
- To increase the intensity of your rowing and to build strength, do "power poppers," short pieces rowed at

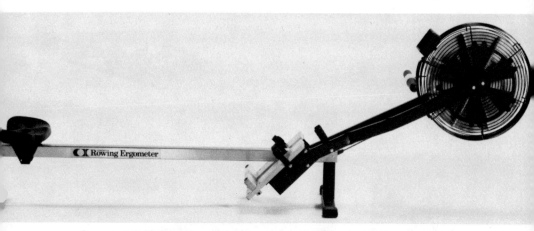

Concept II Ergometer. (Photo courtesy of Concept II)

full power using a higher gear than usual. The rest pieces should be long enough to allow you to row at full pressure during the popper. Try a 20-second popper followed by one minute and 40 seconds of easy rowing. Do 8–10 poppers in a workout and don't do them more than 3 times a week. Be especially careful to warm up before this workout.

- To train for a 5-mile ergometer race, row 8–10 miles steady state. Rowing longer than the race distance will give you added confidence in handling 5 miles. You will have to row slower than you would for a 5-mile race but try to maintain a good steady pace.
- To get a high-quality aerobic workout, row 20 strokes hard and 5 strokes easy for at least 20 minutes. The 5 easy strokes allow you to rest a little without letting your heart rate drop significantly. You also begin to adapt to rowing at higher speeds.

Coffey Racing Shells gives these guidelines to people using their rowing machines:

- *Day 1:* Row easily, working on form for no more than 5–10 minutes, keeping the mph reading well below 30. Monitor your pulse to keep it well below your maximum heart rate (220 minus age).

Indoor Rower™ Coffey Rowing Machine. (Photo courtesy of Coffey)

- *Day 2:* Same as Day 1, only increase the length of the workout by a couple of minutes.
- *Day 3, etc.:* Keep increasing the length and intensity of your workout until you are rowing at least 3–4 times a week and at least 15–20 minutes a session, with your pulse at or near your target rate. Keep the mph fairly constant, never letting it vary by more than 5 mph.

USRowing suggests the following workouts:

- *The basic aerobic workout:* 30 minutes of steady-state work. This is the base on which to improve your aerobic capacity. Anything from 10 minutes and up will help, but a 30-minute workout is more valuable than three 10-minute workouts. Steady-state workouts should be your "bread and butter" workouts. Aim for at least 2–3 times a week.
- *Alternate workouts:* These will help when steady-state workouts become boring. For 10–30 minutes (or more)

alternate between ½ and ¾ pressure. The trick here is to not dip below ½ pressure.

- *Interval workouts:* 6 minutes of work—30 seconds all out (watch form), followed by 30 seconds of easy rowing, repeated 5 times. Can also be done in one-minute intervals with one minute of rest.
- *Increment workouts:* 6 minutes—3 minutes at 75 percent; 2 minutes at 80 percent; one minute at max (watch form).
- *Pyramid workouts:*
  10 strokes hard, 10 easy
  20 strokes hard, 10 easy
  30 strokes hard, 15 easy
  40 strokes hard, 20 easy
  50 strokes hard, 25 easy
  40 strokes hard, 20 easy
  30 strokes hard, 15 easy
  20 strokes hard, 10 easy
  10 strokes hard, 10 easy

To liven up your rowing machine training, you may want to enter an ergometer competition. "Erg" races are held across the country throughout the winter. The typical race distance is 5 miles or 2,500 meters, and most events offer several categories for different age and skill levels. These competitions help relieve the drudgery of indoor training for competitive rowers, and the original ergometer race was organized with just that purpose in mind.

The granddaddy of the erg races is CRASH-B (Charles River Association of Sculling Has-Beens) Sprints, which has also been humbly dubbed by its founders and the rowing community as the "World Indoor Rowing Championships." CRASH-B Sprints was the brainchild of world-class sculler Tiff Wood, who came up with the idea while running stairs to stay in shape. The fun-loving nature of the CRASH-B organizing committee is evident in the details of the competition. The CRASH-B "Master of Mayhem" oversees all protocol and ceremony, which typically includes ice cream, a violin rendition of the national anthem, presentation of the "Fly and Die" award for the fastest first mile, and presentation of the team points trophy, which is "symbolic of world ergometer supremacy." CRASH-B always wins the team points trophy. If they are losing, they change the points system to ensure a victory. Usually, CRASH-B features many top rowers and no rules changes are necessary. The event concludes with the singing of the CRASH-B anthem, "Swing Low, Sweet Chariot."

Despite its lighthearted program, CRASH-B features top-notch competition. The 1985 Sprints had more than 500 participants, including more than 50 Olympic and national-team athletes. Competitors race in heats of 6 on Concept II ergometers. The ergs are hooked up to electronic video boats, which advance across a screen to let the participants and fans know the status of the race. Most ergometer races take place in January or February. You can get erg competition information from USRowing or from ergometer manufacturers, such as Concept II.

If the prospect of a 2,500-meter piece at an erg competition isn't challenging enough for you, you may want to try to row yourself into the *Guinness Book of World Records.* The current world record is held by Robert Wilkes, Jr., who rowed 409 miles in 24 hours. Guinness rules specify that you can rest 5 minutes after each 55 minutes of rowing, and that your attempt be witnessed and documented.

Best Times for 1987 CRASH-B Sprints
Times are for a 2,500-meter piece on a Concept II ergometer.

Veteran Women (40 years and older)	10:51.9
Veteran Men (40 years and older)	7:48.8
Men's Masters (27 years and older)	7:46.0
Women's Masters (27 years and older)	9:48.3
Lightweight Women (135 pounds and under)	9:19.4
Lightweight Men (160 pounds and under)	8:03.6
Women's Open	8:43.2
Men's Open	7:38.8

Benchmark 920 Rower. (Photo courtesy of Benchmark)

ROWING MACHINES ON THE MARKET

Model: Benchmark 920 Rower

Manufacturer: AMF American, 200 American Avenue., Jefferson, IA 50129, (800) 247-3978

Specifications: Flywheel with electronically adjustable resistance.
Height: 25½"; length: 82½"; width: 14"; weight: 79 lbs.
Electronic readout of time, resistance, and calories expended.

Price: $595

Model: Precor 615e

Manufacturer: Precor, 20001 North Creek Parkway North, P.O. Box 3004, Bothell, WA 98041-3004, (206) 486-9292

Specifications: Hydraulic resistance cylinders.
Length: 50"; width: 35"; weight: 35 lbs.
Electronic readout of exercise time, stroke rating, total strokes taken during the

workout. Records average stroke rating and maximum stroke rating for the workout. Also gives total strokes since the first day of use.

Price: $350

Model: Pro Form Regatta

Manufacturer: Pro Form, 8170 SW Nimbus Ave., Beaverton, OR 97005, (800) 348-6477

Specifications: Horizontal flywheel.
Height: 23.5"; length: 71"; width: 22"; weight: 56 lbs. Folds to 10.2" × 58.5" × 22".

Price: $899

Model: Coffey Indoor Rower

Manufacturer: Coffey Racing Shells, 48 East 5th St., Corning, NY 14830, (607) 962-1982

Specifications: Horizontal flywheel.
Length: 80"; weight: 65 lbs.
Electronic readout measures mph, maximum mph, total miles, trip miles, and time of workout. Stores on end.

Price: $595

Model: Concept II Rowing Ergometer

Manufacturer: Concept II, Inc., RR 1 Box 1100, Morrisville, VT 05661-9727, (802) 888-7971

Specifications: Flywheel.
Height: 31"; length: 7'10"; width: 18"; weight: 65 lbs.
Electronic readout of time, strokes/minute, stroke output in watts, total workout in average watts, total distance, or total calories burned. Time and distance intervals can be programmed.

Price: $650

Barb Kirch (left), and Ann Marden on a practice row, Philadelphia, 1986. Marden has represented the U.S. for two years at the World Championships. A single, Kirch was in the Olympic pair in Los Angeles, 1984.

Sunrise on the Connecticut River in Middletown, Connecticut.
Wesleyan University rowers carry their shells to the water.

5
WORKING OUT

It may prolong your life; it relieves stress, helps you sleep better, helps you lose weight, improves your appearance, enhances your creativity, improves your self-image and emotional well-being, increases your mental stamina and alertness, and has no destructive side effects. Not a dream, not a drug, it's exercise, and you can enjoy all of its benefits if you do it regularly. The running craze of the seventies and the ensuing fitness boom have brought the benefits of exercise to the attention of the general public, which now pursues them in Ys, fitness centers, and running tracks across the country.

Exercise will improve your cardiovascular system, and that may prolong your life. Diseases of the cardiovascular system are the number one health problem in the United States. Your cardiovascular system consists of your heart and blood vessels. Their job is to circulate blood, which carries the oxygen that is required by your tissues to perform all bodily functions, from muscle contractions to thinking. Your body performs these functions better when it has more oxygen. Exercise increases the efficiency of your heart by conditioning it to do more work with less effort. Exercise also increases the size and elasticity of your blood vessels, and increases the ability of your muscles and blood to absorb, transport, and use oxygen.

While improvements to your cardiovascular system may add years to your life, other benefits of exercise will make those years more enjoyable. Exercise helps you to burn tension and stress. Chemical reactions that take place during exercise also seem to clear and relax the mind, enhancing its creativity and reception to ideas and solutions to problems. Exercise helps you feel good about yourself and your body. Knowing that you have the discipline to exercise regularly makes you happy with yourself and gives you confidence to apply your willpower in your work or other areas of your life that you want to improve. Seeing your muscles change from flabby to firm and watching your waistline slim also give your self-image a boost. Exercise burns calories and increases the rate at which your body burns them; consequently, exercise will enhance any weight-loss program you undertake. As a rower in his seventies observed, "You can feel so much better; you can enjoy everything so much more if you're in good physical condition."

Not all forms of exercise will produce the results that you need and want. A round of golf, or strengthening exercises such as isometrics and weight lifting will not stimulate your cardiovascular system enough to condition it. To achieve the benefits you desire, you need to do aerobic exercise. Aerobic means "with oxygen," and aerobic exercises are those that use and improve the organs that supply and process oxygen to the body. Some examples of aerobic exercise are rowing, running, swimming, bicycling, and walking.

To achieve cardiovascular fitness benefits, you need to do an aerobic exercise at a sufficient intensity for a sufficient duration and a sufficient number of times a week. Before beginning any exercise program, you should get a complete physical and possibly a stress test, and you should consult

An Undine Barge Club double being followed by a motorboat driven by coach Jim Barker (left), and captain Charlie Murray (with megaphone), and Rob Forman. Rowers are Mike Markman (left) and Gary Oscar.

your doctor to establish reasonable and safe fitness goals for yourself.

Once you have received medical clearance and guidance, you are ready to select an exercise program. Rowing is considered to be one of the best, if not the best, exercises you can do. Dr. Frederick Hagerman, who has done extensive testing of elite athletes and rowers in particular, says, "Based on our research and that of others, rowing ranks among the most physiologically demanding of any aerobic sports, with cross-country skiing being its only parallel." For example, basketball players process 3 to 4 liters of oxygen per minute during a game, while elite rowers process about 6.5 liters per minute during a 2,000-meter race. During competition, a rower's energy output is 36 kilocalories per minute versus 30 kilocalories per minute for cross-country skiers. At rest, your heart pumps about five liters of blood per minute, while during intense rowing, eight times as much blood is pumped through your arteries.

Rowing consumes a great deal of energy and requires so

71

much oxygen because it uses all the large muscle groups. When you row, you use muscles in your arms, shoulders, chest, legs, back, and abdomen. The work of all these muscles forces the cardiovascular system to become more efficient in order to satisfy the oxygen demands of your body. Using these muscles enables you to strengthen and tone your whole body and prevents you from creating muscle imbalances that you may acquire from sports that emphasize only a few muscles. For example, runners emphasize their hamstring muscles and usually have to do some type of weight lifting to build their quadriceps, which tend to be underdeveloped in comparison to their hamstrings.

Another advantage of rowing is that it's a smooth, fluid motion that you do sitting down. This feature saves wear and tear on your joints, which don't have to endure stressful jarring and pounding. Many athletes injured in other sports turn to rowing, which is gentle on feet and knees. Likewise, hospital rehabilitation programs prescribe rowing for cardiac patients to improve coordination, upper-body strength, and general fitness. Rowing is also accessible to people with physical handicaps. Catamaran type of boats enable even people who are paralyzed to row. Doug Herland, who has implemented several programs to introduce rowing to both the mobility impaired and the able-bodied, recalls the thrill of teaching a quadriplegic to row: "The first time I helped a quadriplegic learn to row was in a swimming pool. On the third lap I let go of the oars. As he was rowing along he realized my arms weren't following his anymore. He looked at me and said, 'I'm really doing this.' It was a look of wonder, almost disbelief."

Perhaps the most enticing feature of rowing is the lure of water and the great outdoors. Dr. Hagerman explains: "Rowing and sculling offer the participant the unique opportunity to exercise in an entirely different medium, one that can be strenuous, aesthetic, rhythmic, and relaxing at the same time." Another satisfied rower says: "I can't think of a more complete exercise. It's good for your heart, legs, back, and arms. Nothing is left out. But more important is what it does for your spirit. Whether you are with others or alone, you're half floating, half flying—there's joy."

Joy is found in the rhythmic splashing of the oars, in the artistic patterns of the shell's wake and the pools that trail behind the oars, and in the thrilling glide of the boat across the water.

BEGINNING A WORKOUT PROGRAM

Before you begin your rowing fitness program, you should get a complete physical checkup. A physical is necessary to establish the boundaries of your exercise program. If your heart is healthy and you don't have any medical problems, your physician can give you clearance to undertake a regimen that will build up to vigorous exercise. If you do have any health problems, your doctor can give you guidelines to help you exercise within safe limits. For instance, if you have any heart abnormalities (i.e., a recent heart attack or valve disease), diabetes, high blood pressure, or are extremely overweight, your doctor may rule out certain sports or levels of activity. Your physical should also help you determine your maximum heart rate (how hard your heart can be pushed) and your resting heart rate. These figures will be important in setting up your workouts.

The physical should also help evaluate your flexibility and strength. If you are over 35 or have any of the following conditions, your physical should include a stress test (stress EKG):

- Family history of coronary artery disease
- Diabetes
- Smoking
- High cholesterol
- Obesity
- History of heart attacks, chest pains

The stress test evaluates your heart's performance during maximum effort and detects any abnormalities that don't show up when your heart is at rest. During the stress test, the physician will monitor your heart and blood pressure with electrodes as you elevate your heart rate by riding a stationary bicycle or walking a treadmill. The physician will have you continue to exercise until you reach your predicted maximum heart rate. Your heart will also be monitored during the recovery period to detect any problems that don't show up until then. Once you have obtained a fitness evaluation and a determination of how hard you can push yourself, you should begin your fitness program.

Your fitness program will be more meaningful if you are able to quantify your workouts and measure your progress, and your heart rate is the gauge that will enable you to do this. To condition your heart and establish a good level of fitness, the rule of thumb is that you need to exercise at 75 percent of your maximum heart rate for 20–30 minutes, four to five times a week. With this goal in mind, you need to determine the target heart rate you will establish and maintain during a workout. For example, let's say that you are 25 years old and want to exercise at 60 percent of your working heart rate:

- Step 1: Determine your **resting heart rate**. You can get this information from your physical or you can take your own pulse. Count the pulses at your wrist (radial) or the side of your throat (carotid) for 15 seconds. Multiply that figure times 4. Take your pulse 2 or 3 times to get an accurate figure. Let's say you counted 20 beats in 15 seconds:

    $20 \times 4 = 80$ beats per minute = resting heart rate

- Step 2: Determine your **maximum heart rate**. Your doctor can prescribe this or you can subtract your age from 220 to get an estimated maximum heart rate:

    $220 - 25 = 195$ = estimated maximum heart rate for a 25-year-old person

74

- Step 3: Calculate your **working heart rate**. Your working heart rate is the difference between your maximum and resting heart rates:

  maximum heart rate − resting heart rate = working heart rate

  195 − 80 = 115 = working heart rate

- Step 4: Calculate the **target heart rate** for your workout.

  desired % of working heart rate + resting heart rate = target heart rate

  60% (115) + 80 = 149 = target heart rate

- Step 5: Once you have calculated your target heart rate, row at different levels of intensity to determine how hard you have to row to achieve the desired rate. For instance, row at half pressure for 10 minutes and take your pulse. If it's below 149, increase the pressure and take your pulse again.

Your pulse rate and stroke rate are factors of *intensity*, which is only one of the variables in your workout. The other variables are *duration* and *frequency*. Duration is the length of time you choose to exercise. Frequency is the number of times you exercise a week. You can combine different levels of intensity and different lengths of time to create a variety of workouts that will exercise your cardio-vascular system sufficiently. The relationship between intensity and duration is that if your exercise is less intense, i.e., done at a lower percentage of your working heart rate, you need to exercise for a longer period of time to obtain the same physical benefits. This relationship is illustrated by the table on page 76.

Intensity and duration can be quantified in several units, which enable you to vary your workouts further. Your heart rate is the bottom line in determining intensity; however, in your rowing workout, your target heart rate can be achieved in terms of strokes per minute or pressure rating. In other words, the intensity of your workouts can be quantified in either strokes per minute or as a pressure rating. In rowing, the pressure rating is the degree of force or effort you use to pull the oars through the water. Pressure rating is the fraction of full pressure at which you are working. All-out rowing is classified as full pressure, and all other levels of pressure are defined accordingly, i.e., half pressure or three-quarters pressure. Pressure rating has nothing to do with stroke rating, although you tend to row fewer strokes a minute when you're applying full pressure to the oars. Duration of rowing can be quantified by strokes, time, or distance rowed.

Percent of Maximum Heart Rate	Number of Minutes to Exercise
40%	Not Intense Enough
45%	Not Intense Enough
50%	45:01–52:30
55%	37:30–45:00
60%	30:01–37:30
65%	25:01–30:00
70%	20:01–25:00
75%	15:00–20:00

With all these variables in mind, you can set up a workout several different ways. For instance, you can plan to exercise at 70% of your maximum heart rate for 30 minutes or you can make your goal to exercise at 70% of your max for 5 miles. Likewise, you can strive to row at 30 strokes per minute for 2 miles or for 20 minutes. Quantifying your exercise goals in a variety of ways will help keep your workouts interesting.

Use any of the following formulas to set up a workout that will fit your needs:

_____ % maximum heart rate for _____ minutes

_____ % maximum heart rate for _____ meters or miles

_____ % maximum heart rate for _____ strokes

_____ strokes per minute for _____ meters or miles
_____ strokes per minute for _____ minutes
_____ pressure for _____ minutes
_____ pressure for _____ meters or miles
_____ pressure for _____ strokes

Regarding frequency, your goal should be to build up to at least four or five workouts a week. This frequency is necessary to produce a conditioning effect on your cardiovascular system. Use the above table to set intensity and duration goals for each of your workouts. As your heart rate improves, you will need to gradually increase the intensity and/or duration of your workouts to exercise your heart adequately.

Ease into your fitness program gradually. For instance, during your first workout, don't try to row for 30 minutes at 85 percent of your maximum heart rate. Instead, try rowing for 5 or 10 minutes at 60 or 65 percent of your maximum, and monitor how you feel during and after the exercise. The exercise should induce a sweat and increase your breathing rate; however, you should be able to carry on a conversation while exercising and you should not feel any pain. Your pulse should go above 115. The important thing is to find a starting point you are comfortable with and build up from there by gradually increasing the limits of your exercise. Starting out too hard will tear your body down and be discouraging. If you discipline yourself to begin sensibly, your patience will be rewarded with steady progress.

Being sensible also includes allowing your body to rest. Even elite athletes are discovering the importance of rest and are incorporating more rest days into their training schedules. Take at least one day a week off. Rest gives your body a chance to restore its energy supply. If you find yourself feeling run down, reduce the intensity of your workouts and/or add another rest day.

Proper *warm-up, cool-down,* and *stretching* are the final elements of a complete fitness program. Warming up your muscles thoroughly before your workout will help prevent muscle sprains, strains, pulls, and cramps. A warm-up feels good and enables you to ease into your activity without shocking your system. Your warm-up should consist of light rowing or jogging and stretching. Begin by rowing at light pressure for five minutes or long enough to break a light sweat. If you're using a rowing machine, the resistance should be on an easy setting. After light rowing, do a series of stretching exercises to loosen your muscles and prepare them for strenuous activity. Stretching helps the tissues around your joints remain elastic and strengthens cartilage, ligaments, and tendons, and increases your range of motion.

STRETCHING GUIDELINES

- Relax. Removing your shoes enhances relaxation.
- Ease your body into the stretch position.
- Hold the stretch at a point where you can feel the muscle being stretched but you don't feel any pain. If you feel pain, you are stretching too far.
- As you stretch, relax your body, including your face and neck muscles.
- Do not bounce or make any fast, jerky motions. The stretching motion should be smooth and gentle.
- Release the stretch after 15–30 seconds.

Try the following stretching exercises. Doing them will help you stretch and loosen the muscles you will use in rowing. Numerous books have been written on stretching, and there are hundreds of stretching exercises to choose from. If these exercises are not comfortable for you or you want to do additional stretching, you can select other stretching exercises and put together your own program.

Toe touch—Remember to relax. Set your feet about a foot apart. Let your upper body hang limply. Relax your neck. Don't lift your head. As your flexibility improves, try to put more and more of your hand flat on the floor.

Hurdler—Sit on the floor. Extend one leg straight out in front of you and draw your other leg up so that your knee points away from you and the bottom of your foot is pressed against the inner thigh of your extended leg. Bend from your waist to draw your upper body closer to your extended leg. Hold for 15–30 seconds. Reverse legs and repeat.

Head roll—Roll your head around your neck five times clockwise and five times counter-clockwise. Avoid looking up too much when your head is leaning back because this could irritate your cervical spine.

Arm stretch—Lift one elbow above your head with your hand pointing down your back. Slowly pull the elbow down with your other hand. Hold for 15–30 seconds. Repeat with other arm. This is good for shoulder looseness and stretches from your ribs to your elbow.

Kneeling shoulder stretch—Kneel, then stretch your hands forward on the ground as far as possible. Hold 15–30 seconds, release and repeat. This stretches your shoulders.

V-sit—Sit on the floor with your legs spread in a V. Bend from your waist and reach toward your right foot. Hold 15–30 seconds. Release and reach directly in front of you. Hold 15–30 seconds. Release and stretch toward your left foot. Hold 15–30 seconds.

Knee pull to chest—Lie on your back and gently pull one knee up to your chest. Hold 15–30 seconds. Release and change legs. This increases your flexibility and reach at the catch, and increases lower back and hip looseness.

Side stretch—With your feet a little more than shoulder width apart, grasp one hand with the other and bend to the side. Hold for 15–30 seconds. Repeat to other side. This should stretch your entire side from armpit to thigh. It's also good for flexibility in your ribs and the side of your hip. Avoid leaning forward or back.

Look away—Sit on the floor. Extend one leg straight out. Cross your other leg over the extended leg, placing your foot on floor. Turn your upper body away from the extended leg. Hold 15–30 seconds. Repeat with your other leg. This stretches your side and back.

Calf stretch—Facing the wall, extend your arms and lean against the wall. Keep one foot beneath your body with leg bent. Extend the other leg straight back keeping heel on ground. Lean forward until you feel a stretch in the back of your leg. Hold 15–30 seconds and repeat with your other leg.

Toe Touch. Avoid leaning back onto heels and bouncing. This stretch is good for hamstring looseness, lower-back flexibility, and compression at the catch. Do this for 30 seconds.

Hurdler.

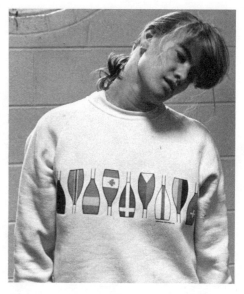

Neck Roll. This exercise is good for sculling, general looseness, and relaxation in the neck and shoulders.

Arm stretch. Avoid overjutting your head and jaw. To increase the stretch, lean sideways from hips toward pulling hand.

Kneeling Shoulder Stretch.

The V-Sit.

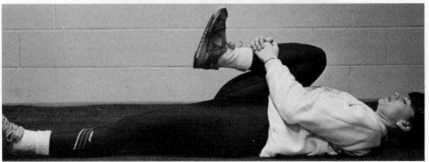

Knee Pull to Chest. A variation is to hold your knee in the crook of your elbow and open the entire leg wider, which will increase the stretch of your butt.

Side Stretch.

Look Away. One leg straight.

Calf Stretch. Point your rear foot at the front foot so you are almost pigeon-toed. Avoid bouncing and turning your back foot out. This exercise is good for flexibility at the Catch and for calf looseness.

THE COOL-DOWN

Cooling down after your workout prevents blood from pooling in your muscles and also helps to remove lactic acid from your muscles. Lactic acid builds up during strenuous exercise and causes soreness the next day if it remains in the muscles. A cool-down should consist of at least five minutes of gentle rowing or jogging. This gentle exercise circulates your blood from your muscles to your heart and also circulates lactic acid out of the muscles. After your cool-down, repeat your stretching exercises. This also helps circulate blood back to your heart and helps you unwind and relax from the exercise. Listening to relaxing music while stretching can enhance your enjoyment and make this routine a highlight of your day.

Document your progress toward your fitness goal by keeping a journal. Recording the facts of your workout, such as heart rate, stroke rate, distance, and time will show how you've improved and help you to plan future workouts. Your log will also help you set goals because it enables you to compete with yourself and try to better your time, distance, or speed. Recording how you felt during your workout will also help you monitor your progress and analyze how your body is responding. If you sustain any training injuries, reviewing your journal may help you find out what workouts might have caused the injury.

Let's summarize the components that you will want to include in your fitness program:

1. Get a complete physical checkup.
    a. If you are over 35 or have risk conditions, the physical should include a stress test.
    b. Find your resting and maximum heart rates.
2. Learn to calculate your target heart rate.
3. Row for 10 minutes at a time, at different stroke rates and pressures to determine the stroke rate and pressure necessary to elevate your pulse to the desired percentage of maximum.

4. Plan workouts with the goal of eventually being able to row at 75 percent of your maximum heart rate for 30 minutes four times a week.
5. Ease into your fitness program. Do your first few workouts at low intensity for only 10–15 minutes. Monitor your heart rate, breathing, and muscles, and increase or decrease the intensity and duration of your workout according to how you feel.
6. Warm up and stretch before you work out:
   a. Do light rowing or jogging for at least five minutes.
   b. Relax; don't bounce or jerk when you stretch.
7. Cool down and stretch after your workout:
   a. Do light rowing for at least five minutes. This circulates blood out of the large muscles and back to the heart. It also removes lactic acid from muscles and helps prevent stiffness and soreness the next day.
   b. Repeat stretching routine.
8. Keep a log to record your progress.

USRowing coaches and athletes offer the following workout suggestions:

Fred Borchelt, 1984 Olympic silver medalist advises the beginning rower to spend the first month of training doing steady rowing at one-half to two-thirds pressure, three times a week. Row at a rate that enables you to converse, and maintain that pace for 20 minutes. Gradually increase the duration until you can row at least 40 minutes at that steady pace. When you can row at least 30 minutes at a steady pace, you can make the workout more interesting by varying the pressure. For instance, row 40 strokes at ½ pressure, then row 10 at full pressure. Then row 35 strokes at ½ pressure followed by 15 at full pressure. Continue the pattern as follows:

> 30 strokes, ½ pressure; 20, full pressure
> 25 strokes, ½ pressure; 25, full pressure
> 30 strokes, ½ pressure; 20, full pressure
> 35 strokes, ½ pressure; 15, full pressure
> 40 strokes, ½ pressure; 10, full pressure

Then repeat the pattern. Continue the cycle for the duration of your workout.

Harry Parker, head coach at Harvard, recommends you spend the first 3-6 weeks of your fitness program rowing at a steady state for 20-60 minutes. Once you build up to 60 minutes, he suggests you time yourself over a set distance and then work to lower your time for that distance.

Harry Parker, competing in the 1985 Head of the Charles. He is presently the head crew coach at Harvard University. In 1960 he was the Olympic singles sculler for the U.S. He has been the national team sculling coach for a number of years, including 1984, when the book The Amateurs *was written.*

John Ferriss, Head of USRowing Coaches Education Program, suggests a workout of rowing hard for one minute, easy for 30 seconds, hard for one minute, etc., and continuing the pattern for 20-25 minutes. Another workout Ferriss suggests is to divide a 30-40-minute workout into three or four 10-minute pieces. Row for 10 minutes at a harder rate than you would row 40 continuous minutes, rest briefly (easy rowing), and then row another 10-minute piece.

Larry Gluckman, head coach at Princeton, recommends workouts of 20–60 minutes at a moderate heart rate to improve general fitness.

BEYOND FITNESS: TRAINING FOR COMPETITION

If you decide to train for competition, you will need to incorporate additional training principles into your program. The first principle that must be introduced is *anaerobic energy.* Anaerobic energy is that energy which your body produces without oxygen. An example of the use of anaerobic energy is running a 100-meter dash. The race is short enough so that your body can produce the necessary energy by burning energy reserves without the presence of oxygen.

To understand the concept of anaerobic energy it is helpful to look at how the body produces energy. Your body uses three different energy systems to create fuel for muscle contractions. All of the systems create ATP, adenosine triphosphate, a compound that is stored in your muscles and provides energy for contractions. The three systems work together to provide energy for the duration of a practice or race. When one system uses up its energy reserves, another system kicks in. The energy systems vary in how quickly and how long they can produce energy from ATP; consequently, the system your body uses to produce energy depends on the intensity and duration of the work it is doing. The systems are classified as aerobic or anaerobic, depending on whether or not they use oxygen to produce ATP.

THE THREE ENERGY SYSTEMS

ATP-PC system (anaerobic)—The ATP-PC system produces immediate energy for 15–20 seconds of intense exercise when you use more oxygen than you can take in.

LA system (anaerobic)—The LA system produces quick (but not as quick as the ATP-PC system) energy for 45–50 seconds of intense effort. The LA system kicks in when the ATP-PC system exhausts its ATP supply. LA stands for lactic acid, which is a by-product of this system. Lactic acid interferes with muscle contractions and is responsible for that leaden, totally exhausted feeling that you get at the end of an all-out sprint. The accumulation of lactic acid in your muscles forces you to either stop the activity or reduce the intensity so that your body can take in enough energy without oxygen for 60–70 seconds. After that you must either stop the activity or slow down so that your oxygen system can take over.

Oxygen system (aerobic)—Your oxygen system produces ATP for steady-state activities in which you are taking in as much oxygen as you are using. The aerobic system supplies more than 90 percent of the energy needed to run a marathon.

Rowing a 2,000-meter race requires the use of both the anaerobic and the aerobic energy systems. At the start of the race you need a quick, intense burst of energy (high stroke rate and pressure), which is supplied by the ATP-PC and LA systems. Because of the accumulation of lactic acid in your muscles, you can't maintain this pace for the duration of the race; you have to level off to a stroke rate and pressure that your body can maintain with the oxygen energy system. Surges during the middle of the race call the anaerobic system back into play, and the energy for the finishing kick during the last 500 meters is also supplied by the ATP-PC and LA systems. To be competitive in a race, you will need to condition both your aerobic and anaerobic energy systems.

TRAINING METHODS

Since rowing is primarily an aerobic activity, you should devote most of your training to developing your endurance, or aerobic capacity. The best way to improve your aerobic system is to train at an intensity just below your *anaerobic threshold*—the point at which your body incurs oxygen debt and switches from the aerobic to the anaerobic energy system. The following types of workouts will condition your aerobic system and increase your endurance:

Steady-state rowing—This type of workout consists of rowing continuously at one-half to three-quarters pressure for 30–60 minutes. Steady-state rowing also enables you to concentrate on your technique.

Alternate—Alternate training consists of rowing continuously at alternating speeds. For instance, you row 20 strokes per minute for 5 minutes, and then increase the rate to 25 strokes per minute for 2 minutes. You can also row at alternating pressures. For instance, 10 minutes at half pressure then 5 minutes at three-quarters pressure. This type of training improves your aerobic capacity and your ability to increase pace and pressure. It is a good alternative to steady-state rowing because it is less boring. You can plan different workouts by strokes, times, or distances, or you can just change pace and pressure spontaneously when you get out on the water.

Over-distance training—This type of training consists of rowing farther than the race distance at a slower than race pace. The benefits are improvement of endurance and confidence in your ability to row the race distance. You should build up to where you can row the distance more than once during the workout. When you do repetitions, row lightly for the same distance between the pieces.

ANAEROBIC TRAINING

The primary route to anaerobic conditioning is interval training. Intervals are a series of alternating pieces of intense rowing and easy rowing (rest). For instance, you might row hard for one minute and then paddle for one minute, and repeat the set five times. Intervals can improve anaerobic and aerobic conditioning, depending on their intensity and duration. Intervals with short rests place more emphasis on the aerobic system, while intervals with long rests work primarily to condition the anaerobic systems. The following chart developed by John Ferriss describes different types of workouts and their benefits.

CHART OF WORKOUTS by John Ferris

	Class of workout	Length of work interval	Quantity of work	Stroke rate range	General quality, heart rate	Rest time (work:rest ratio)	Comments or training effect
SHORT INTERVALS	Stroke play or speed training	15–45 sec. up to 250 m. or 5–30 str.	8–15 min., 1–2 × race or 300–500 str.	Max. rate 36–45 per min.	Above race speed, max. HR	lots of rest (1 : 3)	Lactate production; speed and technique at high ratings
SHORT INTERVALS	Traditional intervals	1–2 min. 300–600 m. 40–70 str.	10–15 min. 2 × race dist. 400–600 str.	Race rate, 30–38 per min.	Near race speed, max. HR	same as work time (1 : 1 or 1 : 2)	Lactate tolerance; oxygen transportation
LONG INTERVALS	Race tempo training	3–7 min. or 1–2 km. or	12–18 min. 2–3 × race	Sub-race to race rate	Race or 170 to max.	3–7 min. (1 : 1 or 1 : 2)	Oxygen transportation; rhythm at race pace
LONG INTERVALS	Broken intervals	7–10 min. e.g., 8 × 40/20 (8 × [40 sec. on, 20 sec. off])	20–30 min. 3 reps.	Below race rate	Near race intensity, max. HR	15–20 sec. and 2–5 min. between reps.	Max. oxygen consumption; oxygen utilization and transportation; race pace rhythm and feel
LONG INTERVALS	Over-distance (AT) training	10–20 min. or 2–5 km.	2–4 reps.	24–32 per min.	Medium, 150–175 (near AT HR max. at end)	5–7 min. (1 : 1/3)	Oxygen utilization and transportation
CONTINUOUS	Alternate training	6–12 min. cycles of changing rate at 80%, e.g., 3/2/1 at 20/24/26	30–60 min	20–32	Medium, 140–160	No rest	Endurance; oxygen utilization; rowing rhythm and technique
CONTINUOUS	Steady state training	No change of speed or pressure	40–90 min.	18–26	Slow, 130–150	No rest	Endurance; oxygen utilization

GUIDELINES FOR TRAINING

Aerobic and anaerobic training is done in different doses, depending on variables such as your fitness level, the race distance, and the preparation time. Use the following guidelines to tailor your training program to your specific needs:

- Until you can row steady state for 40–60 minutes, your training should be entirely aerobic.
- The longer the race distance, the more emphasis you should place on aerobic conditioning.
- A training program is divided into periods classified as the preparation period, the precompetition period, and the competition period. The competition period is the duration of your racing schedule. During the season, strategy, technique refinements, and speed work are emphasized. Workouts tend to be shorter and more intense with more rowing done at racing speed. The precompetition period begins six to eight weeks before the beginning of the season. During this period, emphasis should shift from longer endurance workouts to short speed workouts, which begin to accustom you to racing speeds. The precompetition period is preceded by the preparation period, which emphasizes aerobic training, the development of good technique, and an endurance base.

Victorious University of New Hampshire men's lightweight (160 pounds) eight celebrating their victory at the 1986 Dad Vail Small College Nationals.

6
COMPETITION

Rowing is tough to beat for physical fitness. You'll also find that rowing has a lot to offer as a spectator sport. Large rowing events are called regattas, and some are colorful, festive affairs that you can make an afternoon of. On a nice sunny fall or spring day, take a picnic lunch and enjoy it on the riverbank or lakeshore as you watch the colorful display of crews racing by. You might want to enhance your viewing pleasure by boning up on basic racing rules and procedure. The standard racing distance is 2,000 meters, which is about 1¼ miles and takes about seven minutes for a men's single to row. Regattas sometimes feature races of 1,000 or 500 meters, but 2,000 meters is the distance men and women race in international competition. The course typically has six lanes with markers overhead, on shore, or both. On some courses the lanes are separated by buoys.

Crews compete in heats and semifinals to determine the six finalists. All the boats must be aligned before the referee gives the starting command. Starts sometimes take several minutes because as soon as one boat is lined up, another drifts off course or inches beyond the starting line. At some

93

regattas, stake boats are provided to expedite starts. Each lane has a stake boat and a person on the stake boat holds onto the stern of the shell in his lane to keep it in position until the starting command is given. Some referees will ask each rower if he or she is ready before starting the race. This is called polling the boats. Coxswains (people who steer big boats such as eights and fours) raise their hands to alert the starter if their boat is drifting off course.

When the boats are all in position, the referee gives the starting command in French, "Etes-vous prets? Partez!" (Are you ready? Go!), sometimes accompanied by a gunshot on the word "Partez." If a boat false-starts, the race is restarted. If a crew false-starts twice, it is disqualified. If any of the crews' equipment breaks within the first 30 seconds or 100 meters of the race, the referee will restart it. After a clean start, the referee follows the race in a launch (motorboat) to make sure the boats do not interfere with one another. Boats can stray out of their lanes and not be penalized as long as they don't impede another boat's progress. If a boat drifts off course and looks as if it is going to interfere with another boat, the referee warns the offending boat with a white flag. A red flag from the referee tells the offending boat to stop. Judges at the finish line determine the order of finish, and a white flag is raised if the race was legal and fair. A red flag is raised if one of the competitors files a protest.

During the race, the crews to watch are the ones with seemingly effortless, perfectly synchronized strokes. All the blades should leave and enter the water together, with minimal splash. Less splash indicates a cleaner catch and release. Likewise, the individual sculler who has the smoothest, quietest stroke is likely to be leading the race.

Regattas usually include several different events and classes for people of various ages and experience. Events are divided into sculling and sweep rowing. In sculling events, each rower handles two 9½-foot oars. In sweep rowing, each rower handles one 12½-foot oar. There are three sculling events: single (1x), double (2x), quad (4x). There are five

Temple University's winning men's varsity eight in the 1982 Dad Vail Regatta, Philadelphia. Runner-up is Florida Institute of Technology.

sweep events: Eight w/cox (8+), four w/cox (4+), four w/o cox (4−), pair w/cox (men only) (2+) and pair w/o cox (2−). Rowers are classified by the USRA according to age and weight:

Juniors: You may compete as a Junior until December 31st of the year you turn 18.

Masters: You become a Master the year you turn 27.

Lightweight Men: 72.5 kilogram or 159.84 pound limit.

Lightweight Men's Team boats average: 70 kilogram or 154.32 pound limit.

Lightweight Women: 59 kilogram or 130.07 pound limit. Women's team boats are not averaged.

Some of the most popular events in the country are "head

races," such as the Head of the Charles or the Head of the Schuylkill. Head races differ from regular regattas in that the rowers leave the starting line single file, one at a time 10–15 seconds apart, and compete against the clock rather than directly against the other rowers. A head race makes for daylong viewing of a continuous stream of rowers passing by. In the big head races, the rowers' times are clocked by a computer system that tabulates the final results.

Here is a list of some of the most widely known rowing events:

Harvard-Yale—The Harvard–Yale race dates back to 1852 and is America's oldest intercollegiate athletic event. Each year the crews square off for a grueling four-mile battle on the Thames River in New London, Connecticut. The two schools spend up to a month at their respective training headquarters (Harvard at Redtop, Yale at Gales Ferry) preparing for the intense duel. The race is permeated with tradition and honor, and taken to heart by competitors and alumni alike. When Yale suffered a string of 18 defeats, team pictures of the losing crews were not displayed at Gales Ferry until a victorious crew finally ended the losing streak. As of the 1986 race, the record stands at Harvard 70, Yale 51.

Head of the Charles—The Head of the Charles is one of the most popular rowing events in America. The race is held on the Charles River in Boston and attracts more than 3,000 rowers and 100,000 spectators. Vincent Ventura, who has rowed in every Head of the Charles since 1968, describes the regatta as "one incredible processional." Boats start down the winding three-mile course every 10 seconds for six hours. The race is a favorite of most rowers, who make an annual pilgrimage to the event to reunite with old teammates and friends. Members of the 1972 Olympic silver medal eight reassemble every year to compete in the Head of the Charles.

The Henley Royal Regatta—Established in 1839, the Henley is the Wimbledon of rowing. The regatta is a five-day event held in Henley on the Thames in England. More than 2,000 competitors take part in rowing's social event of the year and more than 100,000 fans watch the spectacle. Many of the spectators come dressed in rowing blazers and straw hats, toting parasols and wicker picnic baskets. China and crystal substitute for paper plates and cups. Currently, Henley does not hold women's events, although in 1981 women were invited to participate. One of the women who rowed in 1981 was Liz O'Leary, Radcliffe's coach. Liz described her impression of Henley: "It's unique, a novelty. There's no other regatta quite like it. It's very social and reflective of an elegant style of living. You see a lot of long dresses and parasols. Their idea of a tailgate party is to put a white linen tablecloth on the back of the Rolls Royce, drink champagne, and watch the boats go by." A favorite

The finish of a lightweight (160 pounds) doubles race at the 1983 Royal Canadian Henley Regatta in St. Catharines, Ontario (near Niagara Falls). The regatta lasts five days and in 1986 comprised 233 heats and 80 finals during 43 hours of racing. It's a rowing addict's dream.

American rowing tale about Henley is that it snubbed legendary Philadelphia oarsman John B. Kelly, Sr., who won three Olympic gold medals. According to the story, the Henley wouldn't let Kelly compete in 1920 because he had worked as a bricklayer. Supposedly, the regatta committee felt that Kelly's occupation might give him too great an advantage over the "gentlemen" competitors. The committee contends that Kelly was rejected because his club had committed some type of rules violation.

The Cincinnati Regatta—Since 1982, the Cincinnati Regatta has been recognized as the men's national intercollegiate championship. The regatta is held at Harsha Lake, just east of Cincinnati. The winning men's varsity eights from the Eastern Sprints, Pacific Coast Championships, IRAs, and the Harvard–Yale race are invited to the regatta, and challengers are also welcomed to vie for the title of national champion.

The San Diego Classic—Held in April, this two-day regatta is the first major event of the rowing season in the United States. The race takes place on Mission Bay and features collegiate, Masters, and Juniors events. Top crews from the previous season are invited to the Classic and receive honorariums to help pay their way. In the past, festivities have included sky divers and balloon races.

National Championships—The first national championships were held by the National Association of Amateur Oarsmen in 1873. The women's national championships were first sponsored by the NWRA in 1964. National Championships for men and women are now held jointly by USRowing.

These regattas and numerous others held across the country are listed in the Regatta Calendar published annually by *American Rowing*.

COMPETING

Chances are, if you've ever sat side by side with another shell and felt the urge to race, you won't be satisfied just to spectate. Peggy O'Neal of USRowing gives the following advice to anyone planning to participate in a regatta:

- If the event is a USRA registered regatta, you must be a USRA member to participate. Write or call USRowing for membership information.
- If possible, arrive for the race a day early so that you can row over the course and become familiar with it.
- If the course isn't buoyed during your practice, row in different lanes to learn what landmarks to steer from.
- Attend the meeting for coaches, coxswains, and blind boats (boats without coxswains). During this meeting information will be given about water hazards and starting commands.
- Check in and get your bow number. Your boat needs to have a bow clip to hold the number. Most racing shells come equipped with number clips and you can buy a set of numbers to fit it. It's a good idea to have a set because in some races you will need to provide your own number.
- Keep track of whether or not the regatta is running on schedule. If it's running behind, take note of how far behind schedule the races are starting.
- Know from memory the three or four events that precede yours.
- Carry a water bottle in your shell, but dump the water before you race.
- Launch 30–40 minutes before your race and do a thorough warm-up that will break a sweat and get you breathing hard. Start rowing with just your hands, then add your back. Row half slide, then three-quarters slide, then full slide. Row 20 strokes at half pressure, 20 at three-quarters pressure, 20 at full pressure. Then row 20 strokes hard, 20 easy; 30 hard, 30 easy; 40 hard, 40 easy. Row five minutes at three-quarters pressure and practice some starts. Continue rowing at half pressure to keep your heart rate up until the start.

- Familiarize yourself with the starter's commands. Know the exact words that he uses and whether he polls the boats or not. Also try to get a feel for how he delivers the commands.
- The referee tries not to start the race until all the boats are aligned. Take little strokes from the catch position to align your boat. From that position you can react quickly to a sudden start.
- If there is a bad crosswind and it is impossible to straighten the boats for the start, the referee may do a countdown start. He will say: "Five-four-three-two-one. Etes-vous prets? Partez!" Competitors time their alignment adjustments during the countdown so that they will be pointed straight down the course on "Partez!"
- If your equipment breaks within the first 30 seconds or 100 meters of the race, the referee will restart it. Jumped slides and open oarlocks don't count.
- Use a series of short strokes at the start. Taking short strokes and not using the full slide enables you to get the boat moving quickly. The following series of strokes make up a typical starting pattern: three-quarters slide, half slide, three-quarters slide, full slide, 15 full-pressure strokes. Then settle into a realistic stroke rate in which you stretch out and relax on the recovery.
- If you are about to stray from your lane and interfere with another boat, the referee will call your lane number and wave a white flag to direct you back to your lane, or hold up a red flag and command you to stop.
- If you feel that the race was unfair for some reason, raise your hand at the finish to protest. A referee will come over to you. If the referee raises a white flag, the race was fair. A red flag means the race is under protest.

STRATEGY

As you become more experienced and competitive, you will want to incorporate some strategy into your races. The following suggested strategies all have their advantages and disadvantages:

Even pace—Most record performances are achieved using this strategy. As the name implies, the idea is to maintain the same pace throughout each segment of the race. You don't exhaust yourself with a dazzling start, nor do you conserve energy during the middle 1,000 meters to save power for a blazing finish. You try to put together your four best 500-meter segments, rowed at the best pace you can maintain over 2,000 meters. The difficulty of this strategy is disciplining yourself not to go out too fast at the start. This means you will usually be rowing at the back of the pack in the first 100 meters or more. Some racers find rowing from behind psychologically difficult. Rowing from behind is also difficult because you can't see your competition.

Rowing in front—The object of this strategy is to get in front and try to stay there. The front-runner benefits by having a view of all his competitors, but he has to set the pace throughout the race and also have enough strength to fight off challenges. Being passed can be devastating and drain a sculler's energy and will.

Surprise strategy—Crews use this game plan to take their competition by surprise. They increase their stroke rate or stroke pressure for a series of strokes to try to blow past another boat. Passing another crew quickly can break them; however, surges can be emotionally and physically draining if they are not successful. Increasing speed by raising stroke pressure is less obvious to the competitors and may enhance the element of surprise. The competition may be able to react quicker to an increased stroke rate. Spurts also increase lactic acid accumulation, which may take its toll at the finish.

Cat and mouse—If you feel that you have a clear advantage over the competition, you can row just fast enough to stay ahead but not drain yourself. Rowers use this strategy in heats to conserve energy for the finals. In heats, some rowers conserve energy further by not rowing to win but just fast enough to get into the finals.

THE OLYMPICS

The Olympics are the pinnacle to which many rowers aspire. Men's rowing has been part of the Olympics since 1900 in Paris, while women's events were added in 1976 in Montreal. The Olympic rowing and sculling program currently consists of the following events:

Men

- Coxed fours
- Double Sculls
- Pairs without coxswain
- Single Sculls
- Coxed Pairs
- Fours without coxswain
- Quad Sculls without coxswain
- Eights

Women

- Coxed Fours
- Double Sculls
- Pairs without coxswain
- Single Sculls
- Quad Sculls without coxswain
- Eights

Currently, the U.S. Olympic rowing teams are selected by a combination of a team selection camp and Olympic trials. The best rowers in the country are invited to attend a training camp where athletes are chosen to row in the big boats, eights and fours. Athletes earn invitations to the camp by winning major regattas during the previous season and by being top performers at the team testing sites. At the testing sites, athletes take several tests, such as an erg piece and weight lifting, to rate their physical abilities and rowing skills.

Small boats such as pairs, doubles, and usually quads, are determined through trials races. Winners of the trials events earn the right to go to the World Championships or the Olympics. The World Championships are the premier competition in every non-Olympic year. They are not held in Olympic years. It usually takes four to six years of intense training and coaching for an athlete to make it to the international level.

Like any dream, the quest for Olympic gold demands

Photograph that hangs in the Vesper Boat Club of the 1964 Vesper Boat Club crew that was the most recent American men's eight to win the Olympics, in Tokyo. From left: First Lt. Joseph Amlong (bow), Hugh Foley, Stanley Cwiklinski, First Lt. Thomas Amlong, Robert Zimonyi (cox), Emory Clark, Boyce Budd, William Knecht, Lt. J.G. William Stowe (stroke). Not shown: Coach Allen Rosenberg.

dedication and sacrifice. The elite rower typically centers his or her life around the sport and has to give up many other experiences. One or two practices a day, in addition to a job, leave little time for anything else. Ginny Gilder, a 1984 Olympian, recalls her training regimen: "I remember being so tired that I couldn't do anything else. I had to pass up a lot of cultural and social opportunities because I would have to go to bed so early to get up for practice in the morning."

Elite rowing also makes heavy demands on the athlete's discipline and willpower. It takes unique determination to get up at 4:00 A.M. on a pitch-black, freezing winter morning and train your hardest for an event that is more than seven months away. Liz O'Leary, a medalist in two World Championships, dealt with the mental challenge by thinking about her competition: "Every time I practiced, I would think, 'What are the East Germans doing today?' and I would work to train harder than they were on that day." World-class rowers also thrive on competing with themselves and discovering new boundaries. O'Leary recalls testing her limits: "Each day I would try to find my limits and see if I could push them higher. I was always striving to lift five more pounds or go a half second faster."

The internal challenge and test of willpower puts tremendous stress on the athletes and sometimes pushes them beyond their physical limits. In preparing for the 1984 Olympic trials, Ginny Gilder trained so hard that she sustained a stress fracture in one of her ribs. In retrospect, she knows that she should have given her body more rest, but she also remembers the fear of forgoing a workout: "I felt that with every workout I missed, I was getting slower."

Most of those who take the trade-offs and make it to the Olympics find that the training and sacrifices were all worth the opportunity to be among the best athletes in the world. In this age of commercialism and politics, you might wonder if the Olympics are still that special, and if the trade-offs are really worth it. Fred Borchelt, a 1984 silver medalist in the eights, explains why the Olympic flame still glows with a magical aura: "For an athlete the Olympics are the pinnacle. The reason the Olympics are so exciting is because you have one chance, one shot. The Olympics are the ultimate because you don't get any better competition. The stakes are higher and people take it more seriously. The competition is very keen, very intense. The eyes of the world are upon you and you are taking part in history."

Perhaps the biggest thrill for Olympians is knowing they are at the top. Borchelt remembers the feeling: "The opening ceremonies were an incredible rush. Being a rower, I wasn't used to cheering crowds. When you get out onto the field, you realize how important it is to give your best. How many people ever make an Olympic team? You realize that you're among the best in the world." Harry Parker, a 1960 Olympian, also remembers the feeling of being a part of

that select group of athletes: "There was less media attention, smaller crowds. The athlete village was small and the
athletes had a sense of togetherness. It was a thrill and an
honor. It was a lot of fun rubbing elbows with the likes of
Herb Elliott and Muhammad Ali."

Doug Herland, 1984 bronze medalist, was awed by the
spirit of the Olympics: "I was amazed by the outpouring of
affection and support. Somebody pushed the fantasy button." For Herland, the finals was one of the magic races.
"There were no glitches. I think of that medal as a gift
because the magic was there. So many times you prepare so
long and hard and then the performance doesn't come
through."

After being on top of the world, world-class athletes face
the challenge of starting new lives when their competitive
careers end. Ginny Gilder notes the difficulty of changing
lifestyles after total immersion in rowing: "After years of
being at the top in what you are doing, it's difficult to do
something new and start out at the bottom again." For Fred
Borchelt, the transition took time as well: "It has taken me
two years to learn that there are other things." Despite the
difficulty of creating a new lifestyle, there was one activity
that Borchelt didn't have to discover. "During the nine
years that I was competing, I never had a chance to go to
the beach in the summer," he says. "When I retired after the
'84 Olympics, I finally had time to go."

Retirement from competition doesn't mean the end of
rowing for world-class athletes. The friendships, loyalty,
and fraternity of rowing sustains athletes throughout their
careers and remains an important part of their lives. The
1972 Olympic silver medal men's eight reunites at the Head
of the Charles every year. Franklin Hobbs, a member of
that team, describes the bond that keeps the crew close:
"Rowing is unique for building friendships. It's exhaust-
ing, and teamwork is everything."

Stained glass in the Undine Barge Club dedicated to Jacob Miller, who rowed 13,395 miles in his lifetime.

7
CLUB ROWING

Clubs are the heart of American rowing and an integral part of many rowers' lifestyles. Club rowing is the vital training ground for many world-class athletes. Clubs provide a social atmosphere in addition to a competitive environment. In the 1950s, Philadelphia clubs had boathouses on the Schuylkill River, as well as upriver houses where dinners, dances, and parties were held after practice or competition. The upriver-house tradition has faded, but rowing clubs continue to be important to rowers. Rowing clubs are the life-support system for competitive rowers. The clubs provide athletes with a place to row, coaching, competition, training partners for those early-morning workouts, camaraderie, and lifetime friendships.

Clubs are especially helpful to a beginning rower. They are a source of experienced, knowledgeable rowers who are eager to help new people get started. Most clubs have a coach or instructor available to give technical instruction. Taking lessons at a club is an excellent way to try rowing before investing in a shell. Most clubs have a variety of shells available for members to rent or use gratis. Clubs usually provide some sort of dock and boathouse for members to use, and some of the larger clubs also have indoor workout facilities.

Joining a club is a perfect opportunity to try out a team boat such as a four or eight. Clubs usually have larger boats on hand and put together crews for local or national regattas. Rowing or sculling with people in a big boat is totally different from sculling in a single. For some rowers, being part of an eight is the essence of rowing. Rowing in perfect synchrony with seven other people is a powerful and euphoric feeling that can addict people to crew. Steven Kiesling, who rowed for Yale, describes the feeling: "When a shell is moving well, when it swings, you feel the strength of all eight rowers at the end of your own oar. That's the euphoria that makes the effort worthwhile."

USRowing has more than 400 clubs across the country. Typical annual club membership dues are less than $150, and some clubs offer a discount for student or family memberships. In some places, new members must pay a one-time initiation fee. Here are some typical benefits to which club members are entitled:

- Use of a dock or other launching facilities.
- Storage space for your personal shell. In some clubs, boathouse space is at a premium, and members must pay rent on top of the membership fee in order to store their shells. Sample rents are $10–$25 a month or $7 a foot per year.
- Use of club shells. Some clubs charge a rental fee.
- Lessons and coaching.
- Use of lockers, showers, indoor training facilities (available at some big, well-established clubs).
- Opportunity to row and compete in team boats.
- Club newsletter subscription.

A FINAL WORD ABOUT GETTING STARTED

For additional information on getting started in rowing, contact USRowing. USRowing is the national governing body that serves all rowers in the United States. USRowing sponsors regional and national championships, and it develops, selects, and funds teams to represent the United States in international competition. USRowing is a clearinghouse of information for rowers, and publishes *American Rowing Magazine* and a wide variety of instructional guides and materials. USRowing also certifies officials and sponsors weekend coaching clinics and an annual weeklong coaching college. The organization has more than 400 club members and 17,000 individual members.

United States Rowing
251 N. Illinois St., Suite 980
Indianapolis, IN 46204
(317) 237-2769

APPENDIX

The following is a list of all the clubs registered with USRowing. Clubs are grouped in alphabetical order by geographic region. For additional information, contact USRowing.

NORTHEAST

Alden Ocean Shell Assn.
Ernestine Bayer
P.O. Box 364
28 Doe Run
Stratham, NH 03885

Alte Achter Boat Club
Peter Raymond
54 Creighton St.
Cambridge, MA 02140

Amherst College R.A.
Attn: Crew Coach
Alumni Gym—Amherst
  College
Amherst, MA 01002

Amoskeag Rowing Club
95 Market St.
Manchester, NH 03101

Aqueduct Rowing Club,
  Inc.
2855 Aqueduct Rd.
Schenectady, NY 12309

Arlington High School
  Crew
Arlington High School
  North
RD 4, Box 263
La Grangeville, NY
  12540

Bates College Rowing
  Assn.
Arnold N. Robinson,
  President
Box 663, Bates College
Lewiston, ME 04240

Beer-Belly Rowing Club
c/o Will Waggaman
38 Terrace Ave.
Riverside, CT 06878

Belmont Rowing Assn.
Tim Wood
350 Prospect St.
Belmont, MA 02178

Berkshire School, R.A.
Jack Stewart, A.D.
Route 41
Sheffield, MA 02157

Blood Street Sculls
Fred Emerson
151 Blood St.
Lyme, CT 06371

Boston Rowing Club
P.O. Box 38
Cambridge, MA 02138

Boston University
Attn: Crew Coach
285 Babcock St.
Boston, MA 02215

Brooks School Crew
Attn: Crew Coach
1160 Great Pond Rd.
North Andover, MA 01845

Brown University
Steve Gladstone
Box 1932, Athletic Dept.
Providence, RI 02912

Buckingham, Browne &
  Nichols
Attn: C. W. Putnam
Gerry's Landing Rd.
Cambridge, MA 02138

Cadet Crew Club
LTC James R. Baker
Dept. of Law
West Point, NY 10996

Cambridge Boat Club
Gerry's Landing Rd.
Cambridge, MA 02138

Camp Pasquaney
Rowing Assn.
Vincent J. Broderick
19 Barrett St.
Needham, MA 02192

Cascadilla Boat Club
Ltd.
P.O. Box 102
Ithaca, NY 14851-0102

Charles River R.A.
Harry Parker
60 J. F. Kennedy
Cambridge, MA 02138

Charter Oak Rowing
Club
Harmon Leete
16 Sycamore Rd.
West Hartford, CT 06117

Chelsea Rowing Club
P.O. Box 22
Norwich, CT 06360

Choate Rosemary Hall
Crew
B. F. Sylvester, Jr.
Choate/Rosemary Hall
Box 788
Wallingford, CT 06492

Citykids Coalition
Rowing
Carl Brown
807 Riverside Dr.
New York, NY 10032

Clark University
Attn: Crew Coach
950 Main St.
Worcester, MA 01610

Colby College Rowing
Assn.
Athletic Dept.
Colby College
Waterville, ME 04901

Colgate Rowing Club
University Club Sports
210 Huntington Gym
Hamilton, NY 13346

College of the Holy
Cross
Attn: Crew Coach
Holy Cross College
Worcester, MA 01610

Columbia University
Ted Bonanno, Crew
Dodge Physical Fitness
Center
New York, NY 10027

Community Rowing,
Inc.
P.O. Box 2604
Cambridge, MA 02238

Connecticut College
R.A.
Connecticut College
Box 1611
New London, CT 06320

Cornell University Crew
Attn: Findlay Meislahn
Teagle Hall—P.O. Box 729
Ithaca, NY 14850

Craftsbury Sculling
Center
Attn: Crew
P.O. Box 31
Craftsbury Common, VT
05827

CRLS Enterprise
Rowing Club
William L. Toomey
6 Buckman St.
Woburn, MA 01801

Dartmouth Rowing Club
Dartmouth College
301 Alumni Gym
Hanover, NH 03755

Durham Boat Club
Jim Dreher
R.F.D. #2 Newmarket
Rd.
Durham, NH 03824

E.A.R.C.
P.O. Box 3
Centerville, MA 02632

East Hampton Rowing
Club
Linda J. Robbins
46 Waterhole Rd.
East Hampton, NY 11937

East Lyme Rowing
Assn., Inc.
Christopher Foster,
Treasurer
P.O. Box 36
East Lyme, CT 06333

Elliot House Boat Club
Hartley Rogers, Jr.,
President
19 Lakeview Rd.
Winchester, MA 01890

Empire State Regatta
Fund
Neil S. Kaye, M.D.
R.D. 1
Voorheesville, NY 12186

Empire State Rowing
Assn.
Thomas Welby
20 N. Broadway
White Plains, NY 10601

Essex Corinthian
Rowing Club
John G. Bogaert
P.O. Box 575
Ivoryton, CT 06442

Exeter Boat Club
Attn: Crew
Phillips Exeter Academy
Exeter, NH 03833

Exeter Rowing Assn.
Richard Tobin
11 Hall Place
Exeter, NH 03833

Fordham Rowing Assn.
Lombardi Memorial
Center
Fordham University
Bronx, NY 10458

Franklin Roosevelt H.S.
Gerald Marquardt, A.D.
South Cross Rd.
Hyde Park, NY 12538

Gloucester Women's
Rowing
Pat De La Chappelle
53 Marmion Way
Rockport, MA 01966

Groton School
Todd Jesdale
Box 991
Groton, MA 01450

Gunnery School Crew
Rick Malmstrom
Rte. 47
Washington, CT 06793

Hamilton College
Greg Selch
Clinton, NY 13323

Hanover Rowing Club
Dartmouth College
301 Alumni Gym
Hanover, NH 03755

Hartford Barge Club
Wayne Hobin
36 Country Lane
East Hampton, CT 06424

Harvard B. S. Boat Club
Student Assn. Office
Kresge/Harvard Business
School
Boston, MA 02163

Harvard Law School
Crew
Matt Teplitz
20 Healey St.
Cambridge, MA 02138

Harvard University
Attn: Harry Parker
60 J. F. Kennedy
Cambridge, MA 02138

Head of the Conn.
Regatta
P.O. Box 1
70 College St.
Middleton, CT 06457

Hobart and William
Smith R.C.
Hobart and William
Smith Colleges
P.O. Box SF93
Geneva, NY 14456

Housatonic Rowing
Assn.
Anne M. Boucher
574 Amity Rd.
Woodbridge, CT 06525

Hull Lifesaving Museum
Ed McCabe, Marine
Skills
24 Fairmount Way
Hull, MA 02045

Hyde Park Rowing Assn.
Ray Barnum
7 Howard Blvd.
Hyde Park, NY 12538

I.R.A.
P.O. Box 3
Centerville, MA 02632

Independence Rowing
Club
Thomas Kudzma
P.O. Box 1412
Nashua, NH 03061

Interlachen Rowing Club
P.O. Box 330
Corning, NY 14830

Iona College Crew
Dennis Lonergan
11 Irving Pl.
New Rochelle, NY 10801

Ithaca College Crew
Ceracche Center
Ithaca College
Ithaca, NY 14850

Kent School Boat Club
Kent School
Kent, CT 06757

Kings Crown Rowing
Assn.
P.O. Box 1263
Bowling Green Station
New York, NY 10274

Knickerbocker Rowing
Club, Inc.
Empire State Plaza
Station
P.O. Box 2249
Albany, NY 12220

Litchfield Hills Rowing
Club
Barbara G. Francis
Box 255, Cathole Rd.
Litchfield, CT 06759

Little Brave Canoe
Rowing Club
Robert Wiley
28 St. Germain St. #2
Boston, MA 02115

Long Beach H.S. Crew
Dr. Tom Patton
Long Beach High School
Long Beach, NY 11561

Manhattan College Crew
Club
Attn: Athletic Dept.
Manhattan College
Bronx, NY 10471

Marist College Crew
McCann Center
Marist College
Poughkeepsie, NY 12601

Mercer County Boat Club
Janet Youngholm
Box 991, Groton School
Groton, MA 01450

Merrimac River Rowing
Assn.
Box 686
Lowell, MA 01852

Merrymeeting Rowing
Club
Douglas Richmond
98 Maine St.
Brunswick, ME 04011

Mid-Hudson Rowing
Assn.
John Mylod
Box 683
Poughkeepsie, NY 12602

Middlesex School
Henry E. Erhard
Middlesex School
Concord, MA 01742

Middletown Rowing
Assn.
Middletown High School
Hunting Hill Ave.
Middletown, CT 06457

MIT Boat Club
Bruce Beall
MIT Branch, P.O. Box D
Cambridge, MA 02139

Morningside Rowing
Assn.
Edward Hewitt
Columbia/Dodge
New York, NY 10027

Mount Holyoke College
Crew
Sharon L. Crow, Athletic
Director
Kendall Hall
South Hadley, MA 01075

Mount Holyoke Women's
Regatta
Vee Wailgum, Assn.
News Director
Mount Holyoke College
South Hadley, MA 01075

Mount Madison Vol. Ski
Patrol
William Barrett
P.O. Box 78/J. W.
McCormick Station
Boston, MA 02101

N.E.I.R.A.
Pete Washburn
Phillips Exeter Academy
Andover, NH 01810

Narragansett Boat Club
P.O. Box 2413
Providence, RI 02906

New Hampshire Rowing
Assn.
Mark Johansen
836 C 31st St. S
Arlington, MA 22202

New Haven Rowing
Club
Norman Thetford
44 Collier Circle
Hamden, CT 06518

New York Athletic Club
c/o Francis X. Sulger
56 Prospect Ave.
Larchmont, NY 10538

New York Rowing Assn.
Michael J. Meehan
215 E. 72nd St.
New York, NY 10021

Noble and Greenough
School
Attn: Crew Coach
507 Bridge St.
Dedham, MA 02026

Nonesuch Oar and
Paddle Club
Phineas Sprague
Prouts Neck
Scarborough, ME 04074

Northeastern University
R.A.
Women's Athletic Dept.,
200 Arena
360 Huntington Ave.
Boston, MA 02115

Northeastern University
Dept. of Athletics
360 Huntington Ave.
Boston, MA 02115

Northfield Mt. Hermon
School
Charles Hamilton
Forslund Gym
Mt. Hermon, MA 01354

Norwalk River Rowing
Club
Susan G. Weinberger
3 Inwood Rd.
Norwalk, CT 06850

NYSU—Maritime
College
Attn: Crew Coach
Fort Schuyler
Bronx, NY 10465

O.A.R.S.
Richard Kline
53 S. Ferry St.
Albany, NY 12202

Oars of Rhode Island
Stephen Peterson
109 High St.
Wakefield, RI 02879

Onota Lake Rowing Club
Peter Wells
P.O. Box 411
Williamstown, MA 01267

Phillips Academy Crew
Attn: Crew Coach
Phillips Academy
Andover, MA 01810

Pioneer Valley Rowing
Assn.
Ferris Athletic Center
Trinity College
Hartford, CT 06106

Pomfret School
Andrew Washburn, Crew
Coach
Pomfret, CT 06258

Riverside Boat Club
Peter Billings
277 Baker Ave.
Concord, MA 01742

Rochester Rowing Club
Ronald Kwasman
41 Vick Park B
Rochester, NY 14607

Rockport Apprenticeshop
Lance R. Lee
Box 539
Rockport, ME 04856

Rude and Smooth Boat
Club
Peter S. Lowe
46 East 91st St.
New York, NY 10128

Sagamore Rowing Assn.
14 Windham Drive
Huntington Station, NY
  11746

Saint Mark's Boat Club
Crew Coach
Southborough, MA 01772

Salisbury Boat Club, Inc.
Art Charles
Salisbury School
Salisbury, CT 06068

Seneca Rowing Club
S. F. Weiskittel
803 S. Main St.
Geneva, NY 14456

Shimmo Rowing Club
Peter S. Heller
237 Park Ave.
New York, NY 10017

Siena College Crew
Jack Mulvey
33 Glendale Ave.
Albany, NY 12208

Simmons College Crew
Sheila Brown, Athletic
  Director
300 The Fenway
Boston, MA 02115

Simsbury High School
  Crew
Simsbury High School
34 Farms Village Road
Simsbury, CT 06070

Skidmore College
P.E. Dept./ Attn: Rowing
  Coach
Skidmore College
Saratoga Springs, NY
  12866

Smith College
Jane Ludwig
Ainsworth Gym
Northampton, MA 01063

South Kent Crew
Attn: Lawrence Smith
  Crew Coach
South Kent School
South Kent, CT 06785

Sparhawk Sculling
  School
Peter Sparhawk
222 Porters Point Rd.
Colchester, VT 05446

Squamscott Scullers, Inc.
D. W. Jones
P.O. Box 526
Exeter, NH 03833-0526

St. Lawrence University
  Rowing
Ted MacMahon
Box 336, SLU
Canton, NY 13617

St. John's High School
Attn: Robert Foley
378 Main Street
Shrewsbury, MA 01545

St. John's University
  Crew
Attn: Crew Coach
Union Tpke. and Utoria
  Pkwy.
Jamaica, NY 11432

St. Paul's School
Attn: Crew
M. R. Blake
Concord, NH 03301

Syracuse Alumni
  Rowing Assn.
C. Roberts
P.O. Box 26
Lockport, NY 14094

Syracuse Chargers
  Rowing Club
Terry W. Korb
4067 Ensign Dr.
Liverpool, NY 13090

Syracuse University
Bill Sanford
Manley Field House
Syracuse, NY 13244

Tabor Academy Rowing
  Assn.
Attn: Crew Coach
Front Street
Marion, MA 02738

Tech Alumni Rowing
  Assn.
John B. Miller
40 Westland Ave.
Winchester, MA 01890

Trinity College
Burt Apfelbaum
Ferris Athletic Center
Hartford, CT 06106

Tufts University
Ken Weinstein
Athletic Dept./Tufts
  University
Medford, MA 02155

Tuxedo Rowing Club
Kurt S. Graetzer
50 E. Orchard St.
Allendale, NJ 07401

USCGA
Attn: Crew Coach
U.S. Coast Guard
  Academy
New London, CT 06320

USMMA Crew
Attn: Crew Coach
U.S. Merchant Marine
  Academy
Kings Point, NY 11024

Union Boat Club
144 Chestnut Street
Boston, MA 02108

Union College Rowing
  Assn.
Ted Eveleth
Box 474, Union College
Schenectady, NY 12308

United Sports Assn. R.C.
395 E. Putnam Ave.
Cos Cob, CT 06807

University of Connecticut
  Crew Club
P.O. Box 762
Storrs, CT 06268

University of Lowell
  Crew
University of Lowell
1 University Avenue
Lowell, MA 01854

University of
  Massachusetts Crew
  Club
Room 9, Totman Gym
Amherst, MA 01003

University of New
  Hampshire
Recreation Sports
151 Field House
Durham, NH 03824

University of Rhode
  Island R.A.
Attn: Head Coach/Crew
Recreation Office,
  Tootell Center, URI
Kingston, RI 02881

University of Rochester
  Crew
Dept. of Sports and
  Recreation
Zornow Center
Rochester, NY 14627

University of Vermont
  Crew
Billings Center
UVM Wills Hall 419
Burlington, VT 05405

Vassar Rowing Club
Scott Sanford, Coach
Browning Rd.
Hyde Park, NY 12538

Warren Rowing Club
c/o McAuliffe
99 Hancock St. #10
Cambridge, MA 02139

Wellesley College Crew
Betsy Cooper
Dept. of P.E. and
  Athletics, Wellesley
  College
Wellesley, MA 02181

Wesleyan University
Donald M. Russell,
  Director of Athletics
Dept. of Physical
  Education
Middletown, CT 06457

West Side Rowing Club
3200 East Blood Rd.
Cowlesville, NY 14037

Williams College Boat
  Club
Williams College
P.O. Box 411
Williamstown, MA 01267

Williamstown Boat Club
Attn: Crew
P.O. Box 411
Williamstown, MA 01267

Winsor Crew
Jennifer Hale
Pilgrim Road
Boston, MA 02215

Worcester Rowing Assn.
F. David Ploss
408 Whitney St.
Northboro, MA 01532

Worcester State Crew
  Club
Student Center
486 Chandler St.
Worcester, MA 01602

WPI Crew
WPI Box 2565
100 Institute Rd.
Worcester, MA 01609

Yale Old Fellows Rowing
  Assn.
James J. Elting, M.D.
R.D. #2 Box 130
Oneonta, NY 13820

Yale University
Crew Office
402 A Yale Station
New Haven, CT 06520

1980 Rowing Club
Holly Hatton
135 Lowell Street
Somerville, MA 02143

MIDDLE ATLANTIC

Alexandria Crew
  Boosters
Kevin Heanue
P.O. Box 3202
Alexandria, VA 22302

American Express
  Rowing Assn.
Sherry Hartigan
SE Corner 16th & JFK
Philadelphia, PA 19102

Annapolis Rowing Club
Roger Frazier, President
29 Decatur Ave.
Annapolis, MD 21401

Bachelors Barge Club
Tully Vaughan
625 Bethlehem Pike
Ambler, PA 19002

Back Bay Viking Rowing
  Club
Bob Garbutt
2 S. Rosborough Ave.
Ventnor, NJ 08406

Baltimore Rowing Club
P.O. Box 10162
Baltimore, MD 21285

Bonner Rowing Assn.
c/o Msgr. Bonner HS
Lansdowne Ave. &
  Garrett Rd.
Drexell Hill, PA 19026

Brigantine Rowing Club
Bob White
613 Woodland Ave.
Absecon, NJ 08201

Bucknell University
  Rowing Club
Janice C. Mueller
Admissions
Lewisburg, PA 17837

Bulldog Rowing Club
c/o Jim Millar
528 Pine St.
Philadelphia, PA 19106

Camden County Rowing
Federation
William Knecht
P.O. Box 1346
Camden, NJ 08105

Camp Dimension
Charles P. Colgan
2106 Bryn Mawr Pl.
Ardmore, PA 19003-2928

Camsis Boat Club
J. Philip Turner
838 South 18th St.
Arlington, VA 22202

Carnegie Lake Rowing
Assn.
Janet Howe
55 Broadripple Dr.
Princeton, NJ 08542

Chester River Rowing
Club, Inc.
R. Stewart Barroll,
President
P.O. Drawer 180
Chestertown, MD 21620

College Boat Club
Bruce Konopka
33rd & Spruce,
Weightman Hall
Philadelphia, PA 19104

Compote Rowing Assn.
Dietrich Rose
4068 Ridge Ave.
Philadelphia, PA 19129

Crescent Boat Club
#5 Boathouse Row
Philadelphia, PA 19130

Dad Vail Rowing Assn.
Jack Seitz
1812 Webster Lane
Ambler, PA 19002

Drexel University Crew
Attn: John Semanik
32nd & Chestnut Streets
Philadelphia, PA 19104

Fairmount Rowing Assn.
Tom Dowd
335 W. State St.
Media, PA 19063

Falcon Rowing Club
Ed Keenan
1217 Filmore St.
Philadelphia, PA 19124

Father Judge High
School
Philip Roche
5336 Saul Street
Philadelphia, PA 19124

Franklin and Marshall
College
Philip L. Calhoun
P.O. Box 3003
Lancaster, PA 17604

Garfield Crew Boosters
Club
P.O. Box 1926
Dale City, VA 22193

George Mason University
Crew
Room 251, Student
Union I
4400 University Dr.
Fairfax, VA 22030

George Washington
University Crew
Attn: Crew Coach
Dept. Intercollegiate
Athletics/Smith Center
Washington, D.C. 20052

Go Row Club
Robert Hyatt
416 River Ave. Ste. 165
Williamsport, PA 17701

Holy Spirit High School
Rev. Michael D'Amico
California and New Road
Absecon, NJ 08201

Hun School of Princeton
William Quirk, Athletic
Director
P.O. Box 271
Princeton, NJ 08542

J. E. B. Stuart H.S.
Attn: Crew Boosters
3301 Peace Valley Lane
Falls Church, VA 22044

Johns Hopkins Crew
White Athletic Center
Homewood, Johns
Hopkins University
Baltimore, MD 21218

La Salle College H.S.
Ken Shaw, Jr.
456 Militia Hill Rd.
Southampton, PA 18966

La Salle University Crew
20th & Olney Ave.
Philadelphia, PA 19141

Lafayette College Crew
P.O. Box 4140
Easton, PA 18042

Lehigh Valley Rowing
Assn.
Steven B. Molder
340 Cattell St.
Easton, PA 18042

Malta Boat Club
Michael L. Brown
59203 Delair Landing
Rd.
Philadelphia, PA 19114

Mary Washington Crew
Club
Box 3774, College
Station
Fredericksburg, VA 22401

Mercyhurst College
Attn: Crew Coach
501 E. 38th St.
Erie, PA 16546

Mercyhurst Prep School
Crew
Attn: Crew Coach
538 E. Grandview Blvd.
Erie, PA 16504

Middle States R.A.
Elizabeth C. Bergen
2834 W. Clearfield St.
Philadelphia, PA 19132

Misery Bay Rowing Club
Stuart J. Miller
1324 South Shore Dr.
#904
Erie, PA 16505

Monongahela Rowing
Assn.
Attn: Crew Coach
P.O. Box 824
Morgantown, WV 26505

N.W.R.A.
Liesel Hud-Broderick
512 West Sedgwick St.
Philadelphia, PA 19119

National Rowing
Foundation
Jack T. Franklin
P.O. Box 6030
Arlington, VA 22206

Navesink River Rowing
Club
P.O. Box 2297
Red Bank, NJ 07701

Northern Virginia R.A.
Col. A.P. Urquia
4009 Harris Pl.
Alexandria, VA 22304

Occoquan Boat Club
John Meehan
P.O. Box 5493
Springfield, VA 22150

Ohio Valley Rowing
Club
Les Pritchard
1800 Washington Ave.
Parkersburg, WV 26101

Old Dominion B.C.
Dee Campbell
203 N. Ripley St. #303
Alexandria, VA 22304

Oneida Boat Club R.A.
c/o Corresponding
Secretary
3 York St.
Burlington, NJ 08016

Penn A.C. R.A.
John J. Ervin, Treasurer
431 Newland Rd.
Jenkintown, PA 19046

Philadelphia Rowing
Program/Disabled
Dorothy Driscoll, Chair
2601 Pennsylvania Ave.
#146
Philadelphia, PA 19130

Phila. Frostbite Regatta
Ken Shaw
456 Militia Hill Rd.
Southampton, PA 18966

Philadelphia Girls
Rowing Club
Attn: Captain
#14 Boathouse Row
Philadelphia, PA 19130

Philadelphia Special
Olympics
Stevens Administrative
Center
13th and Spring Garden
Philadelphia, PA 19123

Potomac Boat Club
Secretary
3530 Water St. NW
Washington, DC 20007

Potomac River Dev.
Center
John P. Devlin
1517 N. Taylor St.
Arlington, VA 22207

Prince William Crew
Assn., Inc.
Woodbridge Chapter
P.O. Box 405
Occoquan, Va 22125

Princeton University
R.A.
Princeton University
Crew
Dept. of Athletics, Box
71
Princeton, NJ 08544

Provident National Bank
William Belden
P.O. Box 7648
Philadelphia, PA 19101

Raritan Valley R.A.
Attn: William T. Leavitt
P.O. Box 1149
Piscataway, NJ 08854

Rutgers University
Attn: William T. Leavitt
P.O. Box 1149
Piscataway, NJ 08854

Scholastic Rowing Assn.
Julian Whitestone
134 Sylvan Court
Alexandria, VA 22304

Schuylkill Navy
4 Boathouse Row
Kelly Dr.
Philadelphia, PA 19130

SMD Rowing Club
Thomas Tranter
St. Mary's Hall-Doane
Academy
Burlington, NJ 08016

St. Andrew's School
Davis Washburn
Middletown, DE 19709

St. Joseph's University
Crew
Bruce Reid, Director of
Student Activities
5600 City Ave.
Philadelphia, PA 19131

Stockton St. College
Crew
Attn: Crew Coach
Stockton State College
Pomona, NJ 08240

Susquehanna Rowing
Assn.
W. C. Smith, President
250 Conway St.
Carlisle, PA 17013

T. C. Williams H.S.
c/o Don Riviere
3330 King St.
Alexandria, VA 22302

Temple University
Gavin White, Crew
   Coach
McGonigle Hall, 047-00
Philadelphia, PA 19122

U.S. Naval Academy
   Crew
Attn: Crew Coach
Annapolis, MD 21402

Undine Barge Club
Carl Viola
730 Byrn Mawr Ave.
Narberth, PA 19072

United States Rowing
   Society
George C. Hines
2058 Poplar St.
Philadelphia, PA 19130

University Barge Club
c/o Secretary
#7 Kelly Dr.
Philadelphia, PA 19130

University of
   Pennsylvania
Weightman Hall (Crew)
Dept. of Intercollegiate
   Athletics
Philadelphia, PA 19104

University of Virginia
   R.A.
Memorial Gym
Charlottesville, VA 22903

University/Baltimore
   Rowing Assn.
Office of Student
   Activities
Charles St. and Mt.
   Royal Ave.
Baltimore, MD 21201

U.S. Dragon Boat Assn.
Jack Seitz
1812 Webster Lane
Ambler, PA 19002

Vesper Boat Club
#10 Boathouse Row
Philadelphia, PA 19130

Viking Rowing
   Foundation, Inc.
Stan Bergman
121 N. Oxford Ave.
Ventnor, NJ 08406

Villanova University
   Crew
G. Tully Vaughan, Head
   Coach
625 Bethlehem Pk.
Ambler, PA 19002

Washington and Lee
   H.S.
1300 N. Quincy St.
Arlington, Va 22201

Washington College
   Crew
Attn: Crew Coach
Washington College
Chestertown, MD 21620

West Potomac Crew
   Boosters
P.O. Box 6211
Alexandria, VA 22306

West River Rowing Club
Pat Anderson
2733 Fennel Rd.
Edgewater, MD 21037

Wharton Business School
Phil Wallis
2318 Spruce St.
Philadelphia, PA 19103

Wilmington Rowing
   Club
P.O. Box 25248
Wilmington, DE 19899

YMCA Three Rivers
   Rowing Assn.
Golden Triangle YMCA
304 Wood St.
Pittsburgh, PA 15222

Yorktown H.S. Crew
Al Villaret
5201 N. 28th St.
Arlington, VA 22207

1789 Sunsetters' Barge
   Club
Willy Packard
3017 Rodman NW
Washington, DC 20008

SOUTHEAST

Alumni Boat Club/
   Rollins College
Kenneth Scott
2762 Sunbranch Dr.
Orlando, FL 32822

American Barge Club,
   Inc.
Aldo F. Berti, M.D.
1321 NW 14th St. #400
Cedars W.
Miami, FL 33136

Atlanta Rowing Club,
   Inc.
Ken Klein
1080 Club Place
Atlanta, GA 30319

Augusta Port Authority
C. Thompson Harley
P.O. Box 2084
Augusta, GA 30903-2084

Augusta Rowing Club
P.O. Box 36
Augusta, GA 30903

Biscayne Bay Rowing
   Assn.
Juan M. Blanes
5801 SW 11th
Miami, FL 33144

Charleston Rowing Club
Attn: Crew
University of Charleston
Charleston, WV 25304

The Citadel Crew
Attn: Crew Coach
Dept. of Physical
   Education
Charleston, SC 29409

Dallas Rowing Club
P.O. Box 7309
Dallas, TX 75209

Duke Men's Crew
P.O. Box 9150 Duke
Station
Durham, NC 27706

Edgewater High School
Martyn Dennis
1324 Indiana Ave.
Winter Park, FL 32789

Florida Institute of
Technology
William K. Jurgens
P.O. Box 1150, Athletic
Dept.
Melbourne, FL 32901

Florida Rowing Centers,
Inc.
Arnold Guy Fraiman
1140 Fifth Ave.
New York, NY 10128

Harbor City Rowing
Club
Billie K. Brown
2900 Riverview Dr.
Melbourne, FL 32901

Jacksonville Episcopal
H.S. Crew
Arthur Peterson, Head
Coach
4455 Atlantic Blvd.
Jacksonville, FL 32207

Knoxville Rowing Assn.
P.O. Box 138
Knoxville, TN 37901

Lookout Rowing Club
Terry Carney
120 McFarland Ave.
Chattanooga, TN 37405

Louisville Rowing Club,
Inc.
Jonathan Newmark
1611 Spring Dr. #5E
Louisville, KY 40205

Mel-Hi Crew Parents
Assn., Inc.
c/o David Tickner
300 Melbourne Ave.
Indialantic, FL 32903

Miami Rowing Club
P.O. Box 490356
Key Biscayne, FL 33149

New Bern Boat Club
Ellis F. Muther
1706 River Dr.
New Bern, NC 28560

Oak Ridge Rowing Assn.
P.O. Box 75
Oak Ridge, TN 37831

Orlando Rowing Club
c/o John R. Ingram
500 Rainbow Dr.
Casselberry, FL 32707

Palm Beach Rowing
Assn.
James K. Green
301 Clematis St., Suite
200
West Palm Beach, FL
33401

Palm Beach Rowing
Club
Edward I. Singer
1460 S. Ocean Blvd.
Manalapan, FL 33462

Port Everglades Rowing
Club
P.O. Box 030071
Ft. Lauderdale, FL
33303-0071

Rollins College
Attn: Crew
P.O. Box 2730
Winter Park, FL 32789

Savannah College of Art
and Design
Richard G. Rowan
342 Bull St.
Savannah, GA 31401

Spring Hill College
Crew
Kathryn Sisterman
4000 Dauphin St.
Mobile, AL 36608

St. Johns Few R.C.
Kris Negaard
1176 Romaine Circle W
Jacksonville, FL 32211

Tampa Rowing Club
P.O. Box 22906
Tampa, FL 33622

Tulane University
Rowing Club
Bob Jaugstetter
209 Tulane University
Center
New Orleans, LA 70118

University of Miami
Joe O'Connor
#1 Hurricane Dr.
Coral Gables, FL 33145

University of Alabama
Crew
Attn: Rowing Coach
University of Alabama
Huntsville, AL 35899

University of Central
Florida
c/o Dennis Kamrad
2763 Sherriff Way
Winter Park, FL 32789

University of Tampa
Bill Dunlap, Crew
Coach
401 W. Kennedy Blvd.
Tampa, FL 33606

University of Tenn. R.C.
Bill McConnell,
President
2106 Andy Holt/Student
Aquatic Center
Knoxville, TN 37996

Viking Crew of LBCC
Robert Bruce Byerly
4901 E. Carson St.
Long Beach, CA 90808

Vista Shores Rowing
Crew
Raoul P. Rodriguez
741 Robert E. Lee Blvd.
New Orleans, LA 70124

Winter Park High School
Bob Mellen, President
2100 Summerfield Rd.
Winter Park, FL 32789

Wolf River Rowing Club
Kemper B. Durand
44 N. Second St. 9th
Floor
Memphis, TN 38103

MIDDLE WEST

Austin Rowing Club
P.O. Box 1741
Austin, TX 78767-1741

Buckeye Rowing Assn.
Nancy Slusarczyk,
President
4200 Royalton Rd.
Brecksville, OH 44141

Chicago River Aquatic
Center
Susan K. B. Urbas
400 E. Randolph St.
#2527
Chicago, IL 60601

Cincinnati Rowing Club
Jill Freshley
P.O. Box 20045
Cincinnati, OH 45220

Columbia Club Crew
Randy Ziraldo
121 Monument Circle
Indianapolis, IN 46204

Creighton University
Crew
2251 Benson Garden, Bv
#2I
Omaha, NE 68134

Culver Military/Girls
Academy
Larry Bess
CEF Box 1
Culver, IN 46511

Cuyahoga Rowing Assn.
Edward W. Ford
2520 Norfolk Rd.
Cleveland Heights, OH
44106

Des Moines Rowing Club
Jamie A. Wade
2300 Financial Center
Des Moines, IA 50309

Detroit Boat Club
Richard Bell
27551 Rackham Dr.
Lathrup Village, MI
48076

Ecorse Rowing Club
P.O. Box 4555
Ecorse, MI 48229

Grand Rapids Rowing
Club
Brian Brewer
P.O. Box 3189
Grand Rapids, MI 49501

Grand Valley Crew Club
Mike Langley
Grand Valley State
College
Allendale, MI 49401

Illinois River Oarsmen
Larry M. Oertley
2207 Daycor Divide
Bartonville, IL 61607

Indianapolis Boat Club,
Inc.
P.O. Box 30339
Indianapolis, IN 46230

Indianapolis USRowing
LOC
Jim McDermott/Barnes
and Thornburg
1313 Merchants Bank
Bldg.
Indianapolis, IN 46204

Iowa Rowing Assn.
Recreational Services
Field House
Iowa City, IA 52242

Kansas State Rowing
Assn.
Mitch Moomaw
Union Activities Center
Manhattan, KS 66506

Kansas University Crew
David Darwin
Dept. Civil Engineering
Lawrence, KS 66045

Lake Phalen Rowing
Assn., Inc.
Doug Holmberg,
President
1858 E. Shore Dr.
St. Paul, MN 55109-4211

Lincoln Park Boat Club
P.O. Box 146345
Chicago, IL 60614

Loyola Academy Rowing
Club
Martin Fahy, Faculty
Sponsor
1100 Laramie
Wilmette, IL 60091

Mariemont Rowing Club
Michael W. Engeman
P.O. Box 9474
Cincinnati, OH 45209

Marietta College Rowing
Assn.
Attn: Crew Coach
Marietta College
Marietta, OH 45750

Mendota Rowing Club
P.O. Box 646
Madison, WI 53701-0646

Michigan Rowing Assn.
Lisa Watt MacFarlane,
President
P.O. Box 7164
Ann Arbor, MI 48107

Michigan State
University Crew
231 IM Sports West
Michigan State
University
East Lansing, MI 48824

Milwaukee Rowing Club,
Inc.
P.O. Box 11171
Milwaukee, WI 53211

Minneapolis Rowing
Club
P.O. Box 6712
Minneapolis, MN 55406

Northwestern University
Crew
Mark Brandewie
2407 Sheridan Rd.
Evanston, IL 60201

Notre Dame Rowing
Club
P.O. Box 55
Notre Dame, IN 46556

Ohio State University
Crew
Jeffrey H. Houston
223 W. 8th Ave.
Columbus, OH 43201

Oklahoma City Rowing
Club
P.O. Box 1937
Oklahoma City, OK
73101

Purdue Crew Club
Recreational Gym
Purdue University
W. Lafayette, IN 47907

Rockford YMCA Rowing
Trahern Ogilby
200 Y Blvd.
Rockford, IL 61107

Sooner Rowing Assn.
Charles W. Oliphant
4400 One Williams
Center
Tulsa, OK 74172

St. Thomas Crew
Ed McCormick
1831 Clinton St. #306
Minneapolis, MN 55404

St. Louis Rowing Club
P.O. Box 16292
St. Louis, MO 65105

Toledo Rowing Club
3600 Summit
Toledo, OH 43611

Toledo Rowing
Foundation
Steven W. Monro/Monro
Steel
2351 Hill Ave.
Toledo, OH 43607

Topeka Rowing Assn.
President
P.O. Box 2423
Topeka, KS 66601

United States Rowing
Assn.
251 N. Illinois St. Suite
980
Indianapolis, IN 46204

University of Texas Crew
Recreational Sports
Gregory Gym 33
Austin, TX 78712

University of Chicago
Crew
c/o Joanne Butler
1143 E. 50th St.
Chicago, IL 60615

University of Michigan
Rowing Club
North Campus
Recreation Bldg.
Ann Arbor, MI 48109

University of Minnesota
Crew Assn.
Men's Crew Program
108 Cooke Hall
Minneapolis, MN 55455

University of Wisconsin
Crew
Attn: Crew Coach
1440 Monroe St.
Madison, WI 53706

University of Minnesota
Women's Crew
238 Bierman Bldg.
516 15th Ave. SE
Minneapolis, MN 55455

Washington University
Crew
Andrew Laine
Washington U. Box 1136
St. Louis, MO 63130

Waterloo Rowing Club
P.O. Box 1435
Waterloo, IA 50704

Wichita State University
Crew
Heskett Center, Box 126
Wichita, KS 67208

Wyandotte Boat Club
P.O. Box 341
Wyandotte, MI 48192

Xavier University Crew
Xavier University
Cincinnati, OH 45207

SOUTHWEST

Balboa Yacht Club
Attn: Rowing Fleet
Chairman
1801 Bayside Drive
Corona del Mar, CA
92625

Berkeley Crew Club
Carol Porter
1880 San Ramon
Berkeley, CA 94707

Cal Poly Crew
Brett Osterfield, Box 325
Active Planning Center/
University Union
San Luis Obispo, CA
93407

California Assn. of
Rowers and Paddlers
Gary Thomas
3610 Sixth Ave.
San Diego, CA 92103

California Maritime
Academy
Attn: Crew Coach
Maritime Academy Dr.
Vallejo, CA 94590

122

California Yacht Club
Rowing
4469 Admiralty Way
Marina del Rey, CA
90292

CSU-Long Beach Crew
Club
Michael Vescovi
4120 E. 8th St., Apt. C
Long Beach, CA 90804

CSU-Sacramento Rowing
Club
Ned Bailey-Troop
2714 Ottowa Ave.
Davis, CA 95616

The Dirty Dozen
Allen H. Trant
4 Commodore #328
Emeryville, CA 94608

Dolphin Swimming and
Boating Club
502 Jefferson St.
San Francisco, CA 94109

Head of the Harbor
Bryan Noyd
P.O. Box 2248
Wilmington, CA 90748

Lake Merritt Rowing
Club
P.O. Box 1046
Oakland, CA 94104

Lake Natoma Rowing
Assn.
David L. Fallis
5712 Moddison Ave.
Sacramento, CA 95819

Long Beach Rowing
Assn.
Attn: Crew
P.O. Box 3879
Long Beach, CA 90803

Los Gatos Rowing Club
22025 Old Santa Cruz
Hwy.
Los Gatos, CA 95030

Loyola-Marymount R.A.
Box 185
7101 W. 80th St.
Los Angeles, CA 90045

Marin Rowing Assn.
Mrs. Joan Corbett,
Secretary
490 Riviera Circle
Larkspur, CA 94939

Mills Cyclone Crew
Kathy Moeller
Mills College
Oakland, CA 94613

Mission Bay Rowing
Assn.
Attn: Executive Director
1001 Santa Clara Pl.
San Diego, CA 92109

Motley Rowing Club
James Willis
4678 Barker Way
Long Beach, CA 90814

Northbay Rowing Club
Greg Sabourin
2390 "I" Street
Petaluma, CA 94952

Oakland Strokes
Pat Lickiss
21 Maple Lane
Walnut Creek, CA 94595

Orange Coast College
Rowing Assn.
Attn: David Grant
2701 Fairview Road
Costa Mesa, CA 92626

Port of Oakland
Whaleboat Crew
James Putz
66 Jack London Sq.
Oakland, CA 94604

River City Rowing Club
726 Adams St. #11
Davis, CA 95616

Rocky Mountain Rowing
Club
Attn: Dave Duval,
President
P.O. Box 6242
Denver, CO 80206

San Diego Rowing Club
P.O. Box 2768
San Diego, CA 92112

San Francisco Police
Athletic Club
Mark E. Hurley
366 Mississippi St.
San Francisco, CA 94107

Santa Barbara City
College
Betsy Zumwalt Perez
321 Arboleda
Santa Barbara, CA 93110

Santa Barbara Rowing
Club
Jan Palchikoff, Coach
University of California/
Robertson Gym
Santa Barbara, CA 93106

Santa Clara University
R.A.
Santa Clara Dept. of
Athletics
Santa Clara, CA 95053

St. Mary's College Crew
Giancarlo Trevisan
15945 Via Cordoba
San Lorenzo, CA 94580

Stanford Crew Assn.
Athletic Dept.
Stanford University
Stanford, CA 94305

Stockton Rowing Club
P.O. Box 2181
Stockton, CA 95201

Tahoe Rowing Club
C'Anne Cook
Box 1835
Crystal Bay, NV 89402

TRW Rowing Assn.
Jimmy Guerrero
One Space Park, 140/
1189
Redondo Beach, CA
90278

UC-Davis Crew
140 Recreation Hall
Davis, CA 95616

UCLA
J. D. Morgan Center/
Men's Crew
405 Hilgard Avenue
Los Angeles, CA 90024

University of California,
Berkeley
Men's Intercollegiate
Athletics-Crew
Harmon Gym
Berkeley, CA 94720

University of California,
Irvine
Attn: Crew Coach
Crawford Hall
Irvine, CA 92717

University of California,
San Diego
Attn: Crew Coach
P.E. Dept. S-005
La Jolla, CA 92093

University of Southern
California Crew
Heritage Hall, Dept. of
Athletics
University Park
Los Angeles, CA 90089

University of the Pacific
Rowing
Tom Kinburg
8307 Solano Ave.
Stockton, CA 95209

Viking Crew of LBCC
Robert Bruce Byerly
4901 E. Carson St.
Long Beach, CA 90808

ZLAC Rowing Club
Attn: Crew
1111 Pacific Beach Dr.
San Diego, CA 92109

NORTHWEST

Bush School Crew
Yiri Zapletal, Coach
405 36th Ave. E.
Seattle, WA 98112

Central Oregon C.C.
Rowing Assn.
Mike Smith, Director of
Student Activities
Central Oregon
Community College
Bend, OR 97702

Conibear Rowing Assn.
Lois Kipper
12105 NE 33rd
Bell, WA 98005

Everett Rowing Assn.
Lori Cummings
Parks and Recreation
3002 Wetmore
Everett, WA 98201

Evergreen State College
Crew
Cath Johnson
Recreation and Athletics
CRC #302
Olympia, WA 98505

George Y. Pocock
Rowing Center
Bruce Thelen
1014 10th St.
Snohomish, WA 98290

Gonzaga University
Rowing Assn.
Rev. Michael Siconolfi,
S.J.
Jesuit House, Gonzaga
University
Spokane, WA 99258

Green Lake Crew
5900 W. Green Lake Way
N.
Seattle, WA 98103

Lake Ewauna Rowing
Club
Robert Anderson
5842 Winter Ave.
Klamath Falls, OR 97603

Lake Washington
Rowing Club
P.O. Box 45117
University Station
Seattle, WA 98145

Lakeside School
Attn: Cabby Tennis
(Crew)
14050 First Ave. NE
Seattle, WA 98125

Lewis and Clark Crew
Athletic Dept.
Lewis and Clark College
Portland, OR 97219

Lute Varsity Rowing
Club
Attn: Crew
Athletic Dept. PLU
Tacoma, WA 98447

Mount Baker Rowing
and Sailing
Seattle Parks and
Recreation
3800 Lake Washington
Blvd. S.
Seattle, WA 98118

OIT Rowing Club
Oregon Institute of
Technology
Klamath Falls, OR
97601-8801

Oregon State Rowing
Assn.
103 Gill Coliseum
Oregon State University
Corvallis, OR 97331

Overlake School
Attn: Crew Coach
20301 NE 108th
Redmond, WA 98053

APPENDIX

Portland Rowing Club
P.O. Box 02370
Portland, OR 97202

Seattle Pacific Crew
Attn: Crew Coach
Seattle Pacific University
Seattle, WA 98119

Seattle Rowing Club
P.O. Box 30003
Seattle, WA 98103

Seattle Tennis Club
Marilyn Start
922 McGilvra Blvd. E.
Seattle, WA 98112

Seattle Yacht Club Crew
Chairman
1807 E. Hamlin
Seattle, WA 98112

Station L. Rowing Club
John T. Booth, President
1724 SE 40th Ave.
Portland, OR 97214

Union Bay Rowing Club
University of Washington
Sports Clubs GD-10
Seattle, WA 98195

University of Oregon
Attn: Crew Coach
EMU Club Sports
Eugene, OR 97403

University of Puget
  Sound
Attn: Crew Coach
1500 N. Warner St.
Tacoma, WA 98416

University of Washington
Crew House
University of
  Washington—GC-20
Seattle, WA 98195

Western Intercollegiate
  Rowing Assn.
Jim Schultz SPU Crew
3414 3rd Ave. West
Seattle, WA 98119

Western Washington
  University
Fil Leanderson, Coach
OM 365
Billingham, WA 98225

Willamette Rowing Club
Frank Zagunis
55 SW Oriole Lane
Lake Oswego, OR 97034

REFERENCES

Brown, Bruce. "How to Select a Rowing Shell." *1986 Rowing Directory*, February/March 1986, 3-7.

Cooper, Kenneth H. *The Aerobics Way*. New York: M. Evans and Co., Inc., 1977.

Cunningham, Francis. "Basic Watermanship: Don't Panic." *American Rowing*, April/May 1986, 26-28.

Cunningham, Francis. "Self Coaching in a Single Scull." *American Rowing*, June/July 1986, 20-23.

Ferriss, John. "Introduction to Sculling." *Rowing USA*, April/May 1985, 25-31.

Ferriss, John (ed.). *Rowing Fundamentals*. National Associatoin of Amateur Oarsmen, 1980.

Hagerman, F. C., and J. E. Falkel. "Defining the Energy Systems." *American Rowing*, October/November 1986, 36-39.

Hagerman, F. C., and J. E. Falkel. "Training the Energy Systems." *American Rowing*, January/February 1987, 40-43.

Hagerman, F. C., and J. E. Falkel. "Rowing for Your Health." *Rowing USA*, August/September 1982, 46-47.

Howard, Ronnie. *Knowing Rowing*. New York: A.S. Barnes and Co., 1977.

127

Kiesling, Stephen. *The Shell Game*. Chicago, Contemporary Books, Inc. 1982.

Kirch, Barbara, et al. *Row For Your Life*. New York: Simon & Schuster, Inc., 1985.

Kita, Joe. "The Oarsman." *Superfit*, Spring 1986, 32–36, 83.

Klavora, Peter. *Rowing One*. Toronto: Canadian Amateur Rowing Association, 1980.

Klavora, Peter. *Rowing Two*. Toronto: Canadian Amateur Rowing Association, 1982.

Kuntzleman, Dr. Charles T., *Rowing Machine Workouts*. Chicago: Contemporary Books, Inc., 1985.

Mendenhall, Thomas C. *A Short History of American Rowing*. Boston: Charles River Books, Inc.

Paris, Jay. "Birth of the Cornfield Regatta." *Ohio Magazine*, June 1984, 59–66.

Peinert, John. "Catch, Drive, Feather, Recover: A Rowing Primer." *Rowing USA*, August/September 1982, 28–31.

Wolf, Julian. "Insuring Your Shell." *Rowing USA*, February/March 1985, 8–10.

Wood, Tiff. "CRASH-B Does it Again!" *Rowing USA*, February/March 1983, 8–10.

INDEX